MW00749299

Maria Christine Moeller (known as Christine) is a multilingual librarian information network specialist who has been interested in her family history from when she was very young. In retirement she had the time to go through the mountains of documents that had been left to her over the years. Through them she was able to discover who her father was. This led to her writing about the course of his life and how the times dictated what his destiny was to be. Christine's own life has been a journey through many countries and continents. She was in five different schools in three different languages before finishing high school. She then went on to do university studies in the United States, France, Switzerland and Austria before entering the services of the Food and Agricultural Organisation of the United Nations in Rome. There she met her husband and they moved to Australia where their two boys were born and where she continued to pursue a career of consultancies in such organisations as the C.S.I.R.O., the Australian Bicentennial Authority, the NSW Bicentennial Council and the NSW Maritime Services Board. She also spent 30 years with the Australia's Special Broadcasting Organisation creating English subtitles for foreign films and documentaries from three of the five languages she speaks. She currently lives in Sydney near one of her sons and divides her time travelling to see her other son in Helsinki and family in Vienna where she was born.

Dedicated to my brother, Peter.
And to my twin sons, Lars and Thor.

This book is also dedicated to all the soldiers who have served or are serving in foreign lands and who have suddenly had to come face to face with their own destinies.

Christine Moeller

Otto Papesch

His Fate of Having Been
Born in Vienna in 1898

Austin Macauley Publishers™
London • Cambridge • New York • Sharjah

Copyright © Christine Moeller 2023

The right of Christine Moeller to be identified as author of this work has been asserted by the author in accordance with sections 77 and 78 of the Copyright, Designs and Patents Act 1988.

All rights reserved. No part of this publication may be reproduced, stored in a retrieval system, or transmitted in any form or by any means, electronic, mechanical, photocopying, recording, or otherwise, without the prior permission of the publishers.

Any person who commits any unauthorised act in relation to this publication may be liable to criminal prosecution and civil claims for damages.

All of the events in this memoir are true to the best of author's memory. The views expressed in this memoir are solely those of the author.

A CIP catalogue record for this title is available from the British Library.

ISBN 9781398410084 (Paperback)
ISBN 9781398410091 (Hardback)
ISBN 9781398403086 (ePub e-book)
ISBN 9781398410107 (Audiobook)

www.austinmacauley.com

First Published 2023
Austin Macauley Publishers Ltd®
1 Canada Square
Canary Wharf
London
E14 5AA

Table of Contents

Family History **14**

Born in Vienna at the Turn of the Century: The Future Looked Promising **23**

The First World War: End of a Carefree Youth **39**

Life Goes on: Otto's Studies and His Chosen Profession **53**

My Father, the Photographer, and the Profession He Pursued His Whole Life Long **61**

1929: My Parents Fall in Love and Wed On 6 June 1931 **74**

World War II: My Father is Once Again Sent to the Front **89**

Additions to the Family: Otto, the Family Man **104**

My Father's Last Years: 1945 to 1947 **114**

Appendices **125**

1. Grebner Papesch Hrdliczka Family Chronicle (Excerpts) *126*

2. My Father's Wartime Diary: 17 February to 12 November 1917 *139*

Recollections of the World War 1914 Begun on 17.2.1917 **140**

18 February 1917, 3 a.m., Graz Railway Station *141*

18 March 1917, Vienna, Schwarzenberg Barracks *141*

18 April 1917 *142*

20 May 1917 *142*

23 May 1917 *143*

26 May 1917 *143*

27 May 1917	*144*
29 May 1917	*144*
1 June 1917	*145*
8 June 1917	*145*
9 June 1917	*146*
11 June 1917	*147*
14 June 1917	*147*
16 June 1917	*148*
20 June 1917	*148*
30 June 1917	*149*
2 July 1917	*149*
16 July 1917	*150*
20 July 1917	*151*
22 July 1917	*152*
25 July 1917	*153*
27 July 1917	*154*
29 July 1917	*154*
2 August 1917	*155*
10 August 1917	*155*
11 August 1917	*157*
15 August 1917	*158*
21 August 1917	*159*
28 August 1917	*160*
25 September 1917	*161*
1 October 1917	*162*
8 October 1917	*162*
12 Novembr 1917	*162*

3. List of Themes *164*

4. List of Drawings *177*

5. My Father's Will *184*

6. Photographic Album of the Invasion of Poland 1939 *185*

7. List of Illustrations *203*

"*Der Herr Ingenieur ist tot, Herr Ingenieur is dead*!" Words the housekeeper yelled out with a trembling voice from the top terrace. I didn't quite understand what it was all about, but I sensed that something terrible must have happened.

Herr Ingenieur, as she used to call him, hadn't yet reached the age of 49 years. He was both in the First and Second World Wars. He was tall and handsome, a courageous man, mondaine and charming. He had a doctorate in photo-chemistry and spent years pursuing his passion of photography. He was Otto Papesch. He was my father.

The news of his passing away reached us on 29 April 1947, my 4th birthday. My grandfather and I were just coming back up from our big garden on the Eichelhof, our family home in the Viennese District of Nussdorf. The garden was laid out over about nine terraces and reached down almost, but not quite, to the shores of the Danube River. The boundary was the little lane extending out beyond the Hackhofergasse. Being close to lunchtime, my grandfather and I were just coming up the steps and when we had reached the bottom of the main terrace, we heard our housekeeper, Frau Max, cry out the terrible message. I felt my grandfather's hand suddenly gripping mine. As I looked up to the tall man that he was, I saw tears roll down his cheeks. His face suddenly turned white. It is still before my eyes today.

My father had been suffering from tuberculosis for quite some time and died on that spring day in the hospital in Lainz. My mother was in the United States at the time. She had left Vienna in October 1946 with the hope of finding a cure that would save her husband's life. She had heard of the drug streptomycin, which was already available there. One can easily imagine her despair as she read the telegram with the news of his death. She became a widow and single parent in one hit, with two small children thousands of miles away. My brother wasn't quite nine years old and I was four.

My father, Otto, was born in Vienna in 1898. His fate was not to be kind to him. He was to witness some of the darkest times of his homeland during not one but both World Wars.

His brother, Viktor, born in 1905, had so much of a better life! He was too young to enter the First World War and later, living in the United States, missed having to enter American military service in the Second World War. In 1940, President F. D. Roosevelt introduced obligatory military training for men in the ages between 21 and 35. Viktor just missed out being called up. Then, from 19 December 1941, when all men between 18 and 64 were called up, Viktor again missed out, probably because of his poor eyesight. Viktor married Mary Marczk in 1934, an American young lady of Slovakian origin, who had been studying music in Vienna. That is where they met. Viktor migrated to the United States and they settled in Chicago. With his PhD in chemistry, he obtained what was to be a lifelong job with G. D. Searle pharmaceutical company. He would become twice as old as his brother, passing away in his late 90s.

After the death of his brother, Viktor wrote to my mother—who was staying with relatives in Vermont at the time—that she should not count on living with or any support from his side of the family. Over the years, he would write his parents a letter now and then and send money, but it was mostly my mother who cared for her parents-in-law. Viktor returned to Austria only once in 1958 and that was for the diamond, the 60th wedding anniversary of his parents. He stayed for only a fortnight.

Otto Papesch at the age of 38 (a rare photo where he is seen smiling), 1936

Family History

My father, Otto Papesch, was born into a cultivated, striving, successful and very close-knit family in the era of the Austria-Hungarian Dual Monarchy. As Virginia Woolf described her own ancestry so beautifully, my father too descended from a great many people—some famous, others obscure.

Peter and Emilie Hrdliczka (my father's maternal grandparents)

The Hrdliczkas originated from a family who managed large estates and their surrounding forests. Marie's parents, Peter Hrdliczka (1818-97) managed the large estate of Count Gudenus in Morawec. His wife, Emilie, née Grebner (1833-1913) was the daughter of Franz von Grebner.

The forefathers of the Grebners date back to the 14th century in Nuremberg. The family crest resembles a Halloween mask and is featured in one of the stained-glass windows of the Catholic, now Lutheran, Church of Saint Sebaldus in Nuremberg. Parts of the family first went to Württemberg. Franz and Thomas, the sons of Württemberg '*Hofrat*' and Treasurer, Franz Christoph von Grebner, later came to Austria with their families in the 17th century. Peter and Emilie had seven children—six sons and one daughter, Marie.

The Grebner family crest in one of the stained-glass windows of the Church of Saint Sebaldus in Nuremberg.

In front, from left to right: Peter, Emilie, Marie and Viktor; Back row from left to right: Paul, Max, Ferdinand, Leopold and Gustav

The von Grebner family crest

My father's parents were related with each other via both their ancestors, the Grebner Family. Otto's great-grandmother, Helene Grebner, was the daughter of Bruno Görgen, neurologist, psychiatrist and senior officer of the mental asylum in Vienna's imperial general hospital. Later, he was to found the Döblinger Private Insane Asylum. One of his most famous patients was the emotionally disturbed poet, Nikolaus Lenau. Helene's biggest pride was to have sung in the choir with Beethoven conducting his last performance of the 9th Symphony in Nussdorf. She hoped that one of her sons would become conductor. Instead, it was to be her great-granddaughter, Gertrude Hoffmann, Viktor Hrdliczka's younger daughter. The Austrian radio, ORF, interviewed her in 1991 and entitled the broadcast, "Der Weibliche Dirigent" [The female conductor: broadcast in Australia on SBS Radio in 1992 and in 1996].

My father inherited some of that musical talent. My mother used to tell me how he would come home after a concert and sit down at the piano and play parts from memory.

Otto's mother, Marie Helene Aloisia-Hrdliczka (1872-1963) had six brothers. One of them, Ferdinand Hrdliczka, was a chemical engineer and founder and managing director of the Herlango firm in Vienna as well as of the firm Lainer & Hrdliczka, where Otto was later to work throughout most of his professional life.

Ferdinand Hrdliczka (Fery) (1860-1942)

My father's uncle, Ferdinand Hrdliczka, founded his firm for the manufacture of celloidin paper in Vienna in 1893. He would later produce other papers as well. In 1913, he merged with the photographic wholesaler, Langer & Co., which became the Vereinigte Photographische Industrien Langer & Comp-F. Hrdliczka. Then, in 1915, it in turn merged with the Goldman camera company and became Herlango Photographic Industries, Proprietary Limited. In 1926, Hrdliczka Herlango became partners with the dry plate and paper manufacturer, Alexander Lainer, under the name of Lainer & Hrdliczka. That was the firm in which my father was to work for many years. One of Fery Hrdliczka's grandsons managed the firm till 1951. The enterprise, Lainer & Hrdliczka, closed down in 1968. Its subsidiary, Herlango, was sold to Niedermeyer Pty. Ltd. in 1992.

My father's other uncle, Viktor Hrdliczka, was a doctor and had a practice in Vienna. He was married to one of the Alder girls, Marie ("Maus"). They had three children—Martha, Viktor and Gertrude (the famous female conductor)—and lived in the 3rd District in Hetzgasse 12.

Viktor Hrdliczka with his wife Marie (née Alder, nicknamed Maus) and their children (left to right) Viktor, Gertrude and Martha

Max Hrdliczka, one of my grandmother's other six brothers, was a specialist in the wood industry and founder of the Impregna A.B. Bystrice pod Hostynem in Moravia and was often in Vienna. He too was married to an Alder girl and so the Papesch, Hrdliczka and Alder families became intimately intertwined. As can be seen in the family photograph taken in 1907, the families often spent Sundays in the park together. The other Hrdliczka brothers lived and worked in Czechia.

Max Hrdlizcka (1865-1958)

The Papesch, Hrdliczka and Alder families in the Prater, 1907. Otto is out on the right beside his father, Ottokar Papesch

Marie Hrdliczka just before her wedding in February 1898

The young Ottokar about to wed his sweetheart, "Maritschi"

Otto's father, Ottokar Thomas Papesch (1868-1960) was *Oberinspektor* in the Austro-Hungarian Bank in Pragerstraβe in Vienna's 3rd District.

Pragerstraβe in the 3rd District seen from the Franzens Bridge

He was the only one of seven siblings who lived in Vienna. All the others presumably lived in or around Prague. I travelled to Prague in 1972 for a meeting as a member of the FAO (the Food and Agriculture Organisation of the United Nations) delegation. I was advised at the time that it would be better not to attempt making contact with any of my relatives there.

Born in Vienna at the Turn of the Century: The Future Looked Promising

The years around 1900 constituted the so-called Golden Age of the Austro-Hungarian Monarchy. Those were years in which culture flourished in all corners of the empire. To quote Virgina Woolf, my father "*descended from a great many people, some famous, others obscure; born into a large connection, born not of rich parents, but of well-to-do parents, born into a very communicative, literate, letter-writing, visiting, articulate late nineteenth-century world...*"

A good sense of humour and positive outlook on life were the very fabric of everyone's day. I found a little notebook among my father's documents with a collection of jokes and witty sentences, which he thought especially funny. My grandfather also liked to crack a joke and had a pun or two up his sleeves at all times. He gave his 12-year-old son a large edition of the humorous book by Wilhelm Busch entitled *Max und Moritz* for Christmas.

Much optimism could be felt everywhere throughout this time. There was a promise of financial and social security and the certainty of being able to achieve a free and happy life created out of self-determination. My father's life was to be altogether a different one from what those early years seemed to herald.

Back to the beginning! My father, Otto Eduard Peter Papesch, was born on 17 November 1898, a frosty day according to the almanac of the time.

1898 Almanac

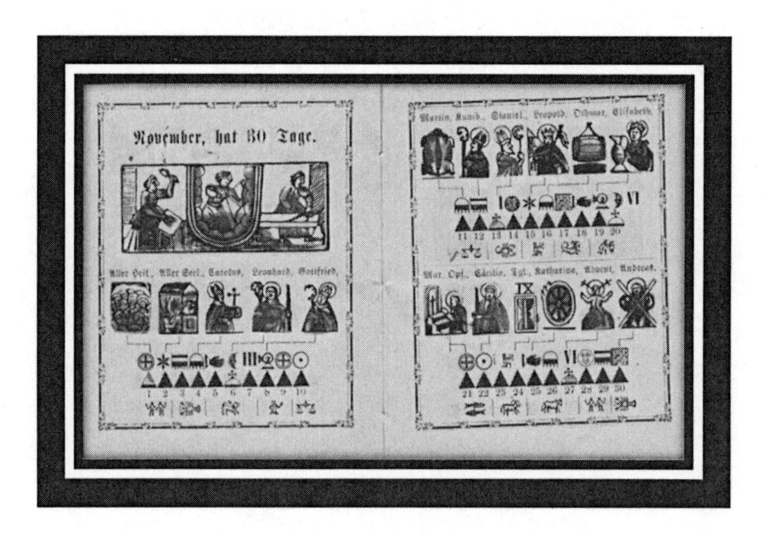

Almanac for November 1898

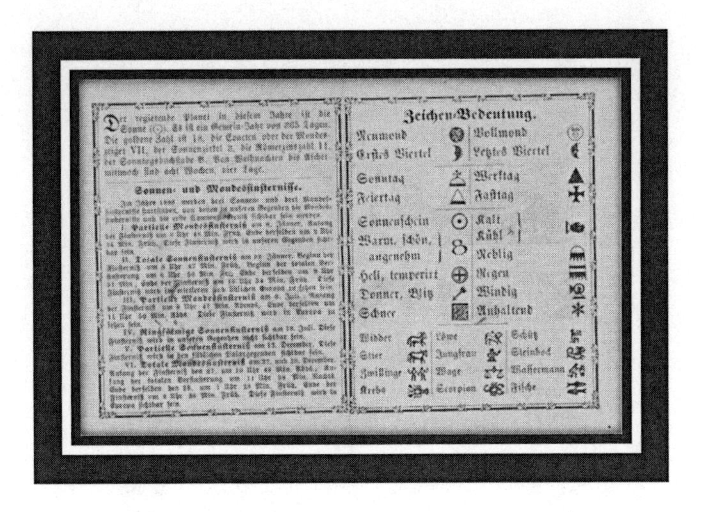

Der regierende Planet in diesem Jahre ist die Sonne (☉). Es ist ein Gemein-Jahr von 365 Tagen. Die goldene Zahl ist 18, die Epacten oder der Mondeszeiger VII, der Sonnenzirkel 3, die Römerzinszahl 11, der Sonntagsbuchstabe B. Von Weihnachten bis Aschermittwoch sind acht Wochen, vier Tage.

Sonnen- und Mondesfinsternisse.

[illegible]

I. **Partielle Mondesfinsternis** [illegible]

II. **Totale Sonnenfinsternis** [illegible]

III. **Partielle Mondesfinsternis** [illegible]

IV. **Ringförmige Sonnenfinsternis** [illegible]

V. **Partielle Sonnenfinsternis** [illegible]

VI. **Totale Mondesfinsternis** [illegible]

Zeichen-Bedeutung.

Neumond		Vollmond	
Erstes Viertel		Letztes Viertel	
Sonntag		Werktag	
Feiertag		Fasttag	
Sonnenschein		Kalt, Kühl	
Warm, schön, angenehm		Neblig	
Hell, temperirt		Regen	
Donner, Blitz		Windig	
Schnee		Anhaltend	

Widder	Löwe	Schütz
Stier	Jungfrau	Steinbock
Zwillinge	Wage	Wassermann
Krebs	Scorpion	Fische

According to this Almanac, it snowed on 17 November 1898,
the day my father was born

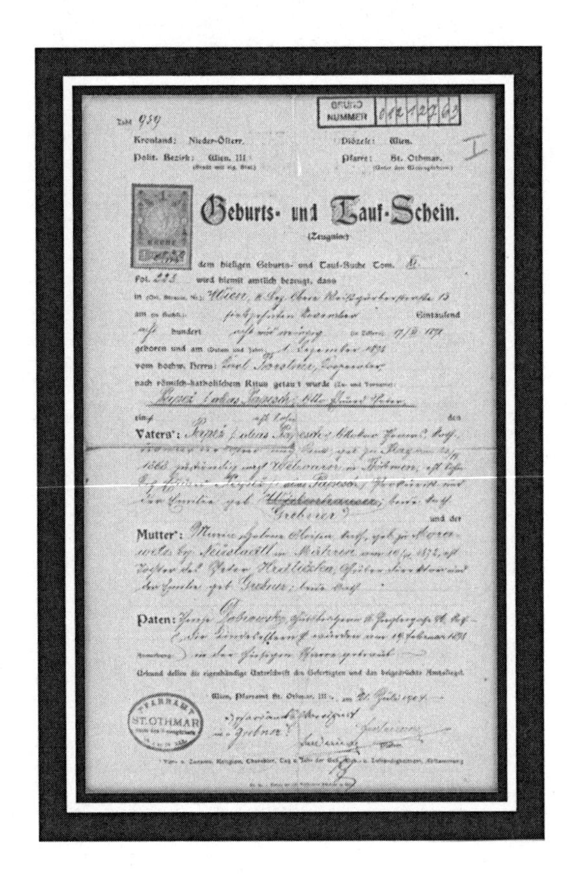

GRUND NUMMER

Kronland: Nieder-Österr. Diözese: Wien.

Polit. Bezirk: Wien. III Pfarre: St. Othmar.

Geburts- und Tauf-Schein.

(Zeugnis)

dem hiesigen Geburts- und Tauf-Buche Tom.

Fol. wird hiemit amtlich bezeugt, dass

in Wien [illegible]

am [illegible] Eintausend

[illegible] hundert [illegible]

geboren und am [illegible]

vom hochw. Herrn: [illegible]

nach römisch-katholischem Ritus getauft wurde [illegible]

[illegible]

des [illegible]

Vaters: [illegible]

und der

Mutter: [illegible]

Paten: [illegible]

Urkund dessen die eigenhändige Unterschrift des Gefertigten und das beigedrückte Amtssiegel.

Wien, Pfarramt St. Othmar, III., am [illegible] 1904

PFARRAMT ST. OTHMAR

My father's birth and christening certificate, 1904

Zahl: 2597
Gau: Wien
Polit. Bezirk: III
Diözese: Wien
Pfarre: St. Othmar
Letzte Post:

Geburts- und Tauf-Schein

(Zeugnis.)

dem hiesigen Geburts- und Tauf-Buche Tom. XI Fol. 223 wird hiemit amtlich bezeugt, daß in (Ort, Straße, Nr.): Wien, 3., Obere Weißgärberstraße 15 am (in Worten): siebzehnten November Eintausend acht hundert neunzigacht (in Ziffern): 17.XI.1898 geboren und am (Datum und Jahr): 1.XII.1898 vom hochw. Herrn: Koop. Karl Forstner nach römisch-katholischem Ritus getauft wurde (Zu- und Vorname): Papesch Otto Eduard Peter ehelicher Sohn des

Vaters*: Papesch Ottokar Thomas, katholisch, [illegible] Beamter, geboren am 23. November 1868 in Prag, nach Welwarn, Böhmen, zuständig; ehel. Sohn des Eduard Papesch, Prokurist, und der Emilie geb. Grebner, beide katholisch,

und der

Mutter*: Maria Helene Aloisia geb. Hrdlicka, katholisch, geboren am 16. November 1873 in Morawetz, Bezirk Neustadtl, Mähren, ehel. Tochter des Peter Hrdlicka, Güterdirektor, und der Emilie geb. Grebner, beide katholisch.

Paten: Therese Dobrowsky, kath. Gutsbesitzerin, ...

Anmerkung: Kindeseltern hier getraut am 19.2.1898.

Urkund dessen die eigenhändige Unterschrift des Gefertigten und das beigedrückte Amtssiegel.

Pfarramt St. Othmar Wien, III.

Wien am 27. September 1938.

Pfarrer

*Vor- u. Zuname, Religion, Charakter, Tag u. Jahr der Geburt, Geburts- u. Zuständigkeitsort, Wohnung.

My father's birth and christening certificate dated 27 September 1938

Otto: 2 months old

Otto with proud mum in 1899

The proud parents with their son, Otto, 1901

And again! Otto with his proud parents, 1901

Otto with his dad, 1902

Otto, 1903

8-year-old Otto, 1906

Otto and his brother Vicki, 1907

Otto and Vicki, 1908

Otto and Vicki, 1909

Ottokar and his sons, Otto and Vicki, in the summer of 1909

Otto and Vicki, 1912

Otto, 1915

The many stories by my mother and my paternal grandparents are testimony to an intimate and loving family life. All members were bound by a love of nature. My grandparents, Ottokar and "Maritschi", often went for long walks in the woods with their sons, Otto and Viktor, or they hiked along the Danube riverbank and went swimming.

Family outing by the river, 1909

Otto, Vicki and their dad sleigh-riding, 1910

My 15-year-old father on horseback, 1913

My father seems to have had a penchant for photography very early on, despite the fact that in 1917, he would write in his diary that he was debating whether to study photography or forestry. In 1914, he wrote a postcard to his grandmother, Emilie Hrdliczka, in which he tells her how much fun he was having with his new camera and how he was looking for subjects in order to enter a photo competition.

My father's postcard to his grandmother Emilie Hrdliczka, 1914

Dearest Grandmama,

Do you recognise the two urchins on this postcard? My camera is great fun and makes me very happy. Is the weather there as bad as it is here? Mr Graf is away for a fortnight. I'm looking for subjects here in order to enter a photography competition. I'm looking forward to seeing Papa. We often go on the search for strawberries which we then eat with cream.

With love to you, Uncle and Aunt,
Your Otto

The building where my father went to school

My father was always keen on sport. In 1913, he received 7 medals during a swimming competition and a medal in discus throwing. Years later, in 1929, he participated in a marathon through Vienna. He was also a member of the Danube Guard.

My father's swimming medals, 1913

My father's swimming medals, 1913 (reverse side)

My father's discus-throwing medal

Marathon through Vienna, 1929

Sport Club: "Donauwacht"

The First World War: End of a Carefree Youth

When Emperor Francis Joseph declared war on Serbia in 1914, thus triggering the outbreak of World War I, it was everyone's opinion that the hostilities would be over quickly and would last no more than a few months. What a dreadful mistake!

Father and mother Papesch took it to be their duty, as did their son Otto, to contribute to the war effort. In unison with the motto, "I give gold for iron", Ottokar and Marie Papesch exchanged their wedding rings for iron ones. The entire population followed suit in order to finance the war.

"I give gold for iron" 1914

My father, Vicki and their mother, 1916

My father with two of his pups

My father, proud in his uniform (my grandfather's chair has travelled with me and currently resides in my home in Sydney, Australia)

Otto was to turn 18 years old on 17 November 1916. He wanted to begin his studies at the Technical University of Vienna in May of that year. Instead, he was 'released' from that programme, of course, in order to enter the Ludovika-Akademie, the military academy in Budapest. My grandparents had to make do with a restricted income since the beginning of the war. It is possible that the prospect of providing their son with free education was behind their decision to send him to the military academy. On the basis of their scholastic grades, volunteers between the ages of 14 and 17 could enter the academy as cadets or 'junior officers' and receive free tuition.

Main building of the Ludovika-Academy in Budapest, 1913

Over 50 postcards and letters from my father to his parents exist from this period in Budapest. In his first letter dated May 1916, he wrote, *I've arrived safely. The trip was really awful. The train moaned and groaned like an old ship so that I almost threw up, but in the end all went well, thank goodness. I left my suitcase at the station and went to the school for volunteers. [...] I went to one this morning and presented myself. All very nice people.*

However, the gear he received didn't fit at all well. He went on to send another letter to his parents soon after. *It took quite some doing before I was able to get the right size cap that fitted my skull. Everything was too small.*

Then he wrote, *I received my uniform today. Just as well that you can't see me or you would faint. The shoes and trousers look the same summer and winter. The coat, shirt, overcoat, etc. all look pretty shabby. Were they taken from dead soldiers? I don't dare go out on the street.*

Those first months in Budapest seemed to be exciting times for my father. He described everything in detail with all the excitement of a joyful young man. This correspondence gives the impression of a certain euphoria, but one can read between the lines that he didn't want to burden his parents with the pain of being separated from them and so, he often hid his own homesickness.

My father apparently fainted when he saw blood or received an injection. He underwent frightful moments of anguish when he had to get his immunisations as prescribed by the military. On 22 May, he wrote his mother, *Injections are to start tomorrow. First, smallpox in the arm. I shall get drunk. Cross your fingers.*

Two days later on 24 May, he again wrote to his mother, expressing his excitement, *Hurrah, hurrah, hurrah, I got my first injection and didn't faint. I got drunk on cognac and black coffee and that helped.*

On 17 June, he went on to describe another episode, *I have just received the cholera and typhus injection. I didn't cop out this time although that would have been easy... I got drunk beforehand with schnapps and that is why I didn't faint. I did feel a bit wheezy afterwards.*

The young cadets had to find their own accommodation in Budapest. Otto found a suitable room only after having visited three others. In his letter to his parents dated May 1916, he even drew a layout.

West Barracks **← Street** **East**

Bed **Table with wash basin/Desk**

Bedside table **----**

Window

Closet

Sofa

Door

West

Linden

Layout of my father's room in Budapest

The young cadets also had to supply their own uniforms. *I shall continue to pester you with what I need for my gear.*

On 14 July, Otto wrote to his father, *Thank you, my dear dad, for the lovely uniform jacket...* Then on 16 July, he went on, *I received the package with the trousers today.*

My father received regular financial support from his family for his sojourn in Budapest. Moneys were transferred securely. After all, Otto's father was Chief Inspector at the Austro-Hungarian Bank and could therefore easily arrange for money transfers for his son. Conscientious as he was, Otto would account for every penny in his letters home.

My father also received regular packages from his family with things he had especially requested from them: coat hangers, toothpicks, soap leaves, cream against lice, a flashlight, a laundry bag, thread, needles, stationery, toilet paper, gloves, a triangle, blotting paper; further: a sheet of white paper, Rembrandt cards Numbers 1 and 2, Rembrandt paper Number 2 and celloidin cards. And then he had another wish. *When you get a chance, 2 pairs of light and 1 pair of heavy socks.*

He was always thankful for every package containing food items, even though he regularly stated that he was getting enough to eat. It appears that my grandmother wanted to send him eggs on one occasion. Edwin Bittman, who was presumably an employee in the household of Papesch-Hrdliczka, wrote the following note in his letter to her dated 16 June 1916, *P.S. The post office just returned the box of eggs with a note stating that an authorisation from the district commissioner is required when sending eggs. I am truly sorry that I am not allowed to send off the eggs.*

It appears that there was more food available in Budapest than in Vienna. My father went to pains to try and find foodstuffs to send to his mother. On 11 October, he asked, *Have you received my two packages of flour yet?* On 13 October, he announced the next one to come: *A 5kg package was sent off today.* During the nine months he spent in Budapest, my father regularly made mention of packages with food items having been sent off: *Has the box arrived?*, *I will be sending another package.*

Life in Budapest seemed to be pleasant for my father. On 5 June, he wrote enthusiastically about his visit to the Széchenyi Thermal Baths. *I went to the Baths yesterday. Fabulous. For 1,20 Kr., you can swim in basins at all different temperatures, the large swimming pool, get a massage or your corns operated on, etc. I was thrilled.*

Széchenyi Thermal Baths in Budapest

It appears that he had quite a lot of free time. On a postcard to his father dated August 1916, he wrote, *By the way, I have always lived lavishly till now. If something is going on somewhere, I'm in it. I have visited all of Pest as well as every restaurant and all of the surrounding regions.*

There was obviously also free time to make music. My father asked his mother to send him a few sheets with notes of the Austrian composer and piano teacher, Czerny. He also asked for the Rondo Capriccioso by Mendelsohn. And on 26 August, he again wrote to his mother with the wish, *[...] if you don't need the sheets from the 'Dreimäderlhaus', please send them to me. There are a couple of Schubert fans here and we whistle his tunes all day.*

However, military training was also the order of the day. My father's first impressions came across as follows: *Things are pretty relaxed around here from what I've seen till now. I thought military life was more regimented. The volunteers went for a hike to Vizegrad yesterday. We are supposed to go on a couple of those every week. No outlook for advancement. People seem to be rather lazy. If you want to be sent into the field, you need patronage!* The meaning of patronage was one of the most frustrating and recurring themes in Otto's correspondence to his parents.

On 2 June 1916, he wrote on one of his postcards, *Please have a look around for patronage. [...] Nothing goes here without patronage. No matter how smart you are, you are bound to fail if you don't have patronage.*

The main courses in military theory that my father had to take at the Ludovika-Academy were tactics and specifically army tactics, weaponry, fortification (battlements), service regulations and field duty. Practical exercises were also part of the course structure. On 14 July, he wrote, *Next week, we will be going on a 3-day marching exercise to Lake Balaton and shortly afterwards on a 3-day camping exercise in the Ofner Mountains* [what are today called the Budai-hegység Mountains, west of Budapest]. *I'm really excited. It should be great.* On 30 September: *We went sharpshooting the other day, I was one of the best.*

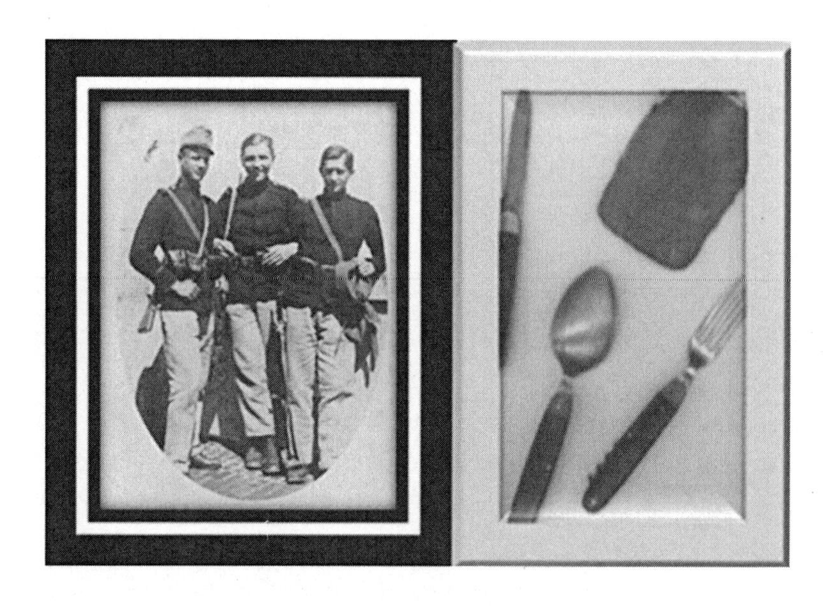

My father with two other fellow cadets, 1916 My father's field cutlery

With the beginning of autumn, the weather started to get cold in Budapest. My father's letters to his parents contained his concerns for the upcoming winter. In October 1916, he wrote to his parents, *It could be that I will be called up this winter, but I am not of feeble health, so that wouldn't be of any concern for me. Millions of people have to suffer it, so I should be able to also.*

I have a letter with a big hole in the middle from about this time that was possibly written on 17 November 1916, the day my father turned 18, or a few days later. You can feel how homesick he was, even though he doesn't say so.

My father had to undergo five days of exams in November 1916. On 27 November, he wrote, *After all of these materialistic studies, I long for some other reading material. I'd like to get my teeth into Plato or Homer... There is an article in the newspaper that we are to get time off for Christmas. I can barely wait for the moment I get off the train on the Ostbahnhof* [the eastern railway station in Vienna]. Then on 3 December, *This was more or less a lazy week. I went swimming several times in the Széchenyi Thermal Baths, a great place.*

It seems that there was considerable confusion about time off during the holidays. On 6 December, my father wrote, *According to orders from the military command, leave entitlements are being withdrawn from all personnel except officers. I don't know why. This is a hard blow for all of us since we wanted to have some fun after all the exams.*

Then on 14 December, *We're beginning to get leave. I don't know for how long. We will get orders this evening. I'm overwhelmed with joy!* My father was hoping for three days leave over Christmas and perhaps a couple of days more to cover travelling time. In the end, he was able to spend the holidays with his family in Vienna.

My father returned to Budapest after Christmas and to his daily routine there. On 5 January 1917, he wrote, *I went to the cinema today and saw the coronation* [of Emperor Karl]; *wonderful pictures and very interesting.* Then on 10 January, *Can you imagine? It wasn't enough that our overtime got withdrawn, we now have to come to school every day from 6.30 to 8.30 and go over military theory under the instructions of a lieutenant and this until the day of the practical exams. Seldom does misfortune strike only once. I hope the exams are soon behind me. These extra hours are quite useless. Everyone is asleep. It's enough to pull your hair out.*

The training period finally came to an end. On 30 January 1917, my father wrote, *Dearest parents. I successfully passed the exams. We are all being sent into the field on 8 February.* Then on 31 January, *Just got news, we are allowed to choose our artillery battery and which theatre of war to go to. I put myself down for the most modern artillery pieces (we are all getting sent to those stations) on the Russian or Albanian front.*

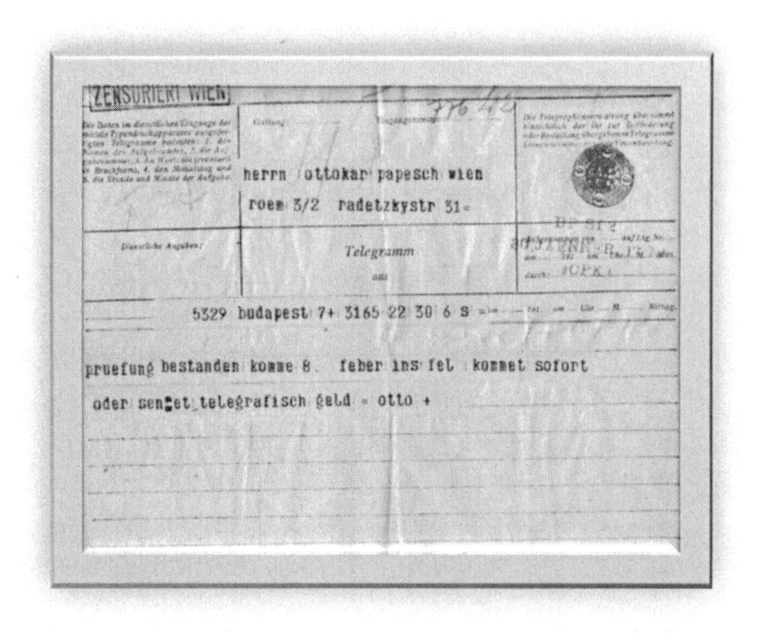

ZENSURIERT WIEN

herrn ottokar papesch wien

roem 3/2 radetzkystr 31 =

Telegramm

aus

5329 budapest 7+ 3165 22 30 6 S

pruefung bestanden komme 8. feber ins fel kommet sofort

oder sen?et telegrafisch geld = otto +

Telegram dated 3 February 1917 to Otto's parents: "Exams successfully passed. Being sent into the field on 8 February. Come quickly or send money via telegraphic transfer. Otto"

And so, my father was finally being sent off to war. He began a diary in February 1917 and noted his farewell from his parents, *Taking leave of my parents was to be on a foggy February morning. They were both very brave and I think I was also, even though I had a lump in my throat.*

The Austro-Hungarian army was ill-equipped for the extent of this war. There were many problems, like the lack of supplies and equipment and delays in the deployment and concentration of troops. My father often mentioned these problems in his correspondence with his parents and later in his diary. The first trip from Vienna to Graz lasted 19 hours! He noted in his diary, *Lord, help us find an express train!* And then, *We were given only bread, and little of it.*

My father was then back in the Schwarzenberg barracks in Vienna where he was handed over to the training of the 31st mortar battery. He was returned to his company in May 1917. His diary entry on 20 May 1917 states that, *After24 hours of a hasty departure, we arrived in Maros Vasarhely* [in those days Transylvania, Romania].

The Romanian landscape made a profound impression on my father. *I'm sitting on the open Lora in order to see this wonderful land first-hand. There is something enchanting about this Transylvania. Undulating hills at the bottom of the Alps line the horizon as the surrounding region becomes ever more mountainous.*

On 30 May 1917, my father's regiment arrived in Berezk [Bereşti], near today's frontier with Moldova. The entries in his diary describing the surrounding landscape indicate that they arrived in the triangle between Tirgu-Mureş, Bereşti and Stanic.

Map of Romania

Supplies arrived relatively regularly. On 16 July, he wrote that he finally had a full belly. On 22 July, his regiment arrived in Stanic where there was a more intensive skirmish with Russian troops. Here, my father was to be confronted for the first time with the realities of war. On 27 July 1917, he would write in his diary, *In our battery, the first casualties. It touches one in a very singular way. People with whom you spoke only a little while ago and who were looking forward to peace just as you were are now cold and stiff under the earth. I was hit by a small piece of shrapnel yesterday. It only damaged my jacket, but it certainly was a* memento mori. *I later had the feeling as if a skeletal hand had touched my shoulder!* Then, on 7 August, he wrote, *This constant closeness with death can really affect one's mood.*

The big offensive lasted for the entire month of August 1917. However, my father was thinking of his life after the war even during those difficult days. He was debating what he wanted to study, either forestry like his Uncle Max or photography like his Uncle Fery. He reached his decision on 2 August. It was to be photo-chemistry! His keen photographic eye was already visible in how he described what he saw: *From our hilltop you got a wonderful view of the battlefield. The enemy positions were bathed in shimmers of magnesium.* On 28 August, the diary entry was, *I have made contact with my future patron, Uncle Fery, and will passionately study photo-chemistry while dreaming of a happy future. [...] I just hope to get back home safe and sound. I don't care about anything else.*

Home and his studies had to wait a while longer, however. The diary entry of 25 September 1917 described his disappointment: *Bad news arrived just now. All the cadets have to serve longer. No longer for 4 months but for 8 instead! No hope for my advancement. With any hope, that might be by August 1918. I'm absolutely desolate. Why does fate punish me in this way and so severely? Enough for now. I shall try to overcome this blow. The demoralising part of it all is that nothing can make the slightest difference. Goodbye Diary, for a long while.*

I have not found any correspondence between my father and his parents during the period between the end of September and November 1917. My grandparents would have surely kept each and every letter and postcard as they did all others. I have often wondered whether that could have been due to postal services not functioning or whether my father was experiencing an emotional or mental breakdown.

According to his diary, my father was still in the vicinity of Berezk at the beginning of October 1917. He mentioned that he had now finally reached the grade of *Fähnrich* or officer candidate and that he had been sent to Brassó as provisions supply officer. Therefore, he must have still been stationed in the Carpathian Mountains. He was made *Fähnrich* and provisions supply officer on 8 October 1917, not mine thrower. Thank goodness, as he put it.

The last entry into his diary was made on 12 November 1917; in other words, five days before his 19th birthday. At that point, my father didn't know where he would be sent to next. But then, *Before you know it, you're in with the cadres.* His journey would take him to Krakow and back to Budapest. After "four bleak days", he was in Vienna again, half a day in Straβnitz and lastly on holiday for

17 days. My father didn't want to stay with the cadres for long: *there's no one I know there; but where to and when?* Those were the last words in his diary. No correspondence with his parents or any diary entries after that.

My father with "Big Bertha"

My father near the bridge of the Brenta River

World War I: my father (left in second row) with his troop. I don't know where.

My father was already back in Vienna in October 1918. According to my grandfather, his main residence was registered to be Radetzkystraβe 31/11/12 on the 10th of that month. It is not clear why my father was discharged early from the military. According to my grandmother, her son returned home with a severe case of pleurisy. He apparently had spent a night under a bridge with another soldier in freezing conditions and completely drenched. Had my grandmother not looked after him day and night with all the care she did, it was very likely he would have died. The experience of war at the front must have landed this courageous young man a heavy blow, both physically and mentally.

The physical conditions of numerous Austrians were absolutely terrible in 1918. The victims of war suffered from stiff joints and paralysis as a result of bullet wounds, the murderous Spanish flu and also from other pandemics. However, a majority of victims suffered from various forms of tuberculosis. In their book entitled "Tuberkulosebekämpfung im Wandel der Zeit" [The Fight Against Tuberculosis Through the Ages], Ermar Junker and Gerhard Wallner wrote that, "*In 1916, when the Austrian Association for the Fight Against Tuberculosis was founded, university professor Hofrat Ritter Jaksch von Wartenhorst pointed out that 540,000 soldiers had succumbed to tuberculosis due to the war.*"... "*After World War I, Vienna became the metropolis of tuberculosis in Austria. It was coined with the name of the Viennese Disease.*"

Life Goes on: Otto's Studies and His Chosen Profession

Otto (22 years old) and Vicki (16 years old), 1920

After his return from the war, my father continued his studies in chemistry at the Technical University of Vienna. He passed his first state exam in 1920.

My father had already become a member of the Photographic Association of Vienna in 1919. His professor in photochemistry and photographic theory at the Technical University, Dr Josef Maria Eder, was a member there as well.

TECHNISCHE HOCHSCHULE IN WIEN.

Formular a

Matrikel-Nummer 391/17

Prüfungsprotokoll-Nummer 80 ex Juli 1921

Chemisch-technische Schule.

STAATSPRÜFUNGSZEUGNIS.

(Erste Staatsprüfung.)

Herr Otto Papesch

aus Wien N. Ö.

wurde auf Grund des an der Staatsrealschule in Wien III erworbenen Reifezeugnisses vom 4. Mai 1916 als ordentlicher Hörer an der Technischen Hochschule in Wien immatrikuliert und hat an dieser Hochschule in den Studienjahren 1917/18, 18/19, 19/20 die zur ersten Staatsprüfung an der Chemisch-technischen Schule vorgeschriebenen Gegenstände besucht.

Auf Grund der umstehend im Auszuge aus dem Prüfungsprotokolle zusammengestellten Erfolge hat der Kandidat gemäß der Verordnung des bestandenen k. k. Ministeriums für Kultus und Unterricht vom 24. März 1912, RGBl. Nr. 59,

die erste Staatsprüfung

an der Chemisch-technischen Schule

— bestanden. —

WIEN, am 7. Juli 1921.

FÜR DIE STAATSPRÜFUNGSKOMMISSION:

Der Dekan der Chemisch-technischen Schule

[Signature]

Vorsitzender.

Auszug aus dem Prüfungsprotokolle

Nachgewiesene Erfolge

Vorprüfungsgegenstände	Noten
Warenkunde und technische Mikroskopie	
Enzyklopädie des Hochbaues	
Wahlfächer: Chemie der Nahrungs- und Genußmittel	
Wahlfächer: Technische Mykologie	
Wahlfächer: Agrikulturchemie	
Wahlfächer: Elektrochemie	

Praktische Staatsprüfung	gut

Gegenstände der theoretischen Staatsprüfung	Note, von der Staatsprüfungs-Kommission festgesetzt	
	auf Grund der vorgelegten Zeugnisse über Einzelprüfungen	nach dem Ergebnisse der mündlichen Prüfung
Analytische Chemie	gut	
Chemische Technologie anorganischer Stoffe	gut	
Chemische Technologie organischer Stoffe	sehr gut	

Die Beschlüsse wurden mit Einhelligkeit der [illegible] Stimmen gefaßt.

Wien, am 23 November 192[illegible]

Der Vorsitzende:

[illegible signature]

[illegible] theoretische Prüfung [illegible] auf Grund des [illegible] des k. k. Ministeriums für [illegible] Unterricht vom [illegible] 1911, Zahl 1996 [illegible]

Excerpts from the examination report, First State Exam, Technical University, Vienna, 1921

TECHNISCHE HOCHSCHULE IN WIEN

Prüfungsprotokoll-Nummer 105/35 Chemisch-technische Schule

Staatsprüfungs-Zeugnis

(Zweite Staatsprüfung)

Herr Papesch Otto

geboren im Jahre 1898 zu Wien in Nieder Österreich

hat in den Studienjahren 1917/18, 1918/19, 1919/20, 1920/21, 1921/22 die technische Hochschule in Wien als ordentlicher Hörer besucht,

und in der Zeit vom ... bis zum 14. November 1922

die praktische Prüfung ~~und am heutigen Tage vor der unterzeichneten Prüfungskommission die theoretische Prüfung~~ abgelegt.

Auf Grund der umstehend im Auszuge aus dem Prüfungsprotokolle zusammengestellten Erfolge hat der Kandidat gemäß der Verordnung des bestandenen k. k. Ministeriums für Kultus und Unterricht vom 24. März 1912, RGBl. Nr. 59,

die zweite Staatsprüfung

an der **Chemisch-technischen Schule**

— bestanden —

und ist sonach auf Grund § 1 der Kaiserlichen Verordnung vom 14. März 1917, RGBl. Nr. 130, zur Führung der **Standesbezeichnung „Ingenieur"** (Ing.) berechtigt.

Wien, am 23 November 1922

Der Vorsitzende der Staatsprüfungskommission:

[signature]

Prüfungskommissäre:

[signatures]

Second State Exam, Technical University, Vienna, 1917/18-1921/22

My father worked as a chemical engineer in the family firm of 'Herlango' between 1 July 1921 and 31 December 1925. He was in charge of the section for celloidin and baryte papers and the production of chemical components. He later became head of the section for photographic plates (see letter from Lainer &

Hrdliczka of 1 March 1938 in which it also states that he left the firm on 1 March 1938).

He received a Heimatschein (certificate of family origin), the precursor of the certificate of citizenship, on 10 October 1924. His title on that document read Ing. Otto Papesch, indicating that he hadn't obtained his doctorate yet.

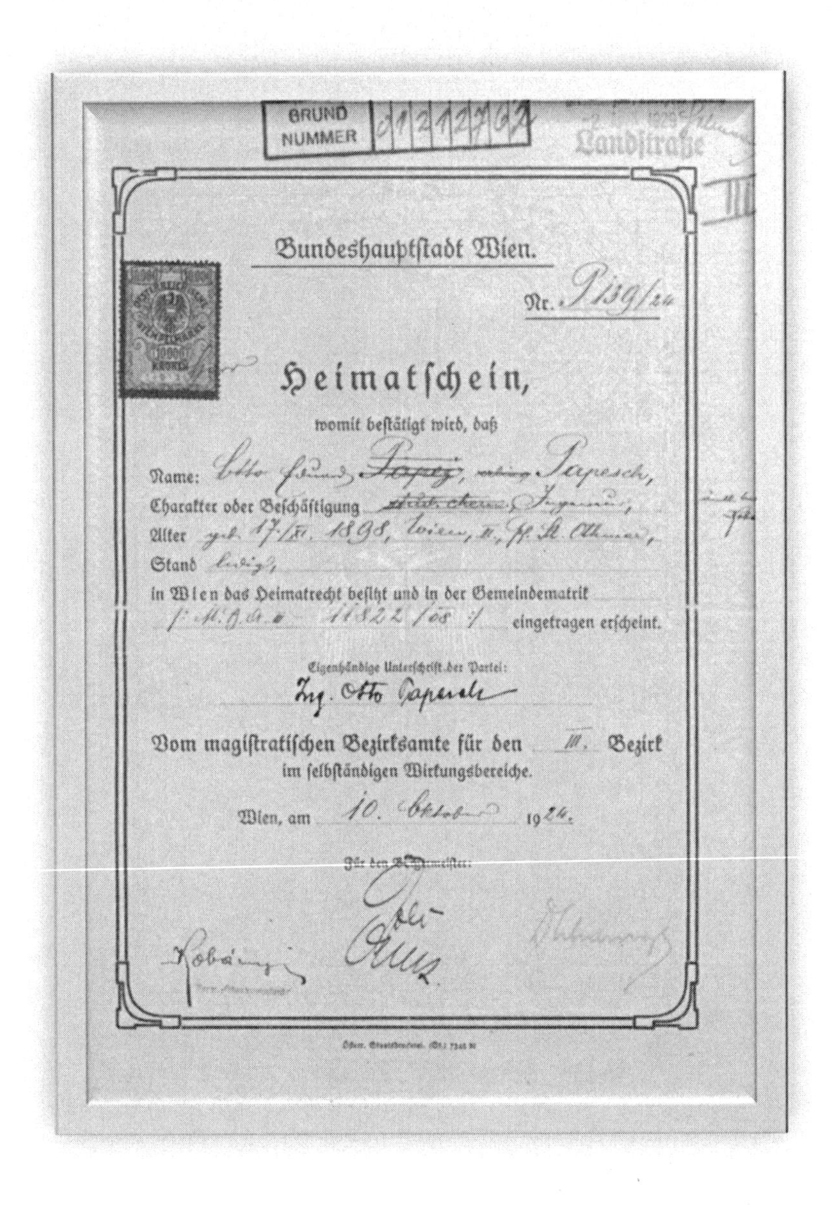

GRUND NUMMER

Landstraße

Bundeshauptstadt Wien.

Nr. P.159/24

Heimatschein,

womit bestätigt wird, daß

Name: Otto ... Papesch,

Charakter oder Beschäftigung Ingenieur,

Alter geb. 17/XI. 1898, Wien, III., Pf. St. Othmar,

Stand ledig,

in Wien das Heimatrecht besitzt und in der Gemeindematrik ... eingetragen erscheint.

Eigenhändige Unterschrift der Partei:

Ing. Otto Papesch

Vom magistratischen Bezirksamte für den III. Bezirk im selbständigen Wirkungsbereiche.

Wien, am 10. Oktober 1924.

Für den Bürgermeister:

Ing. Otto Papesch, Homeland certificate, 1924

K. k. Technische Hochschule in Wien.

Rigorosen-Journal Nr. 328

Name des Kandidaten

Studienzeit

Thema der Dissertation

Gesuch vom Rektorate übernommen am

Datum	
	Die Dissertation den Herren Professoren ... als Referenten übergeben. Frist zur Erstattung des Referates
	Das Gutachten der Referenten erhalten. Dasselbe lautet auf
	Beschluß des Professorenkollegiums über die Dissertation auf
30. X. 1924	Verkündigung des Ausspruches über die Dissertation an den Kandidaten
	Ablegung des Rigorosums. Mitglieder der Prüfungskommission und Abstimmung:

Name:					
		sehr gut			
Unterschrift:					
	der. Dekan	Referenten			Prüfer

Ausspruch der Prüfungskommission

Die Akten an das Rektorat zurückgestellt

Eingetragen!

Wien, am ____/____ 19__

Universitätsarchiv der TU Wien

My father's attempt at obtaining his doctorate failed in 1924

My father worked on his doctoral thesis, *Űber die Reifung von Bromsilber mit Ammoniak und Ammoniumkarbonat* [On the Ripening of Silver Bromide with Ammonium and Ammonium Carbonate] under Professor Eder, his so-called 'Doctorate Dad'. Dr Eder co-founded and developed modern photography and experimental photo-chemistry. The following were some of his groundbreaking discoveries! The development of dry gelatine plates (instead of wet celloidin plates), research into sensitometry, the introduction of chlore brome silver emulsions into the copy process and orthochromatic sensitisation.

Ich bestätige,dass Herr Dr.Ing.Otto Papesch (Wien) in den Jahren 1924 und 1925 seine Doktordissertation "Ueber die Reifung von Bromsilber mit Ammaniak und Ammoniumkarbonat" in dem von mir geleiteten Photochemischen Laboratorium der Graphischen Lehr-und Versuchsanstalt in Wien ausgearbeitet hat und dass diese Dissertation volle Anerkennung fand. Dr.Papesch hat in der Folge die Weiterentwicklung und Praxis auf dem Gebiete der Photochemie und den Nebengebieten stets verfolgt und ist in beiden Hinsichten sehr gut ausgebildet.Er ist seit langem in der Photoindustrie in leitender Stellung wissenschaftlich und organisatorisch tätig und hat für die Fachindustrie immer eine sehr wertvolle Kraft bedeutet.

Wien,am 29.November 1937.

— HOFRAT —
PROF. DR. J. M. EDER
WIEN, III., HAUPTSTRASSE 98
TELEFON U 18-7-44

Letter dated 29 November 1937 certifying that my father worked on his thesis under the guidance of Dr J. M. Eder between 1924 and 1925

My father finally finished his studies in 1926 at the age of 27. I wonder whether he resented the fact that his younger brother had already obtained his doctorate three years earlier.

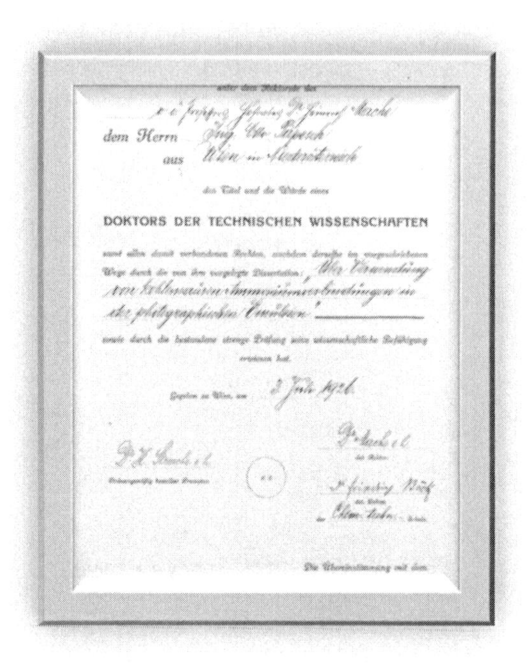

dem Herrn
aus

DOKTORS DER TECHNISCHEN WISSENSCHAFTEN

My father's doctorate certificate, 3 July 1926

A proud "Herr Doktor" strolling down the street, 1926

My Father, the Photographer, and the Profession He Pursued His Whole Life Long

As already mentioned, my father spent most of his professional years working in the firm his uncle Ferdinand Hrdliczka had founded, 'Herlango', and later Lainer-Hrdliczka. In his last years, he was to work for Wien Film.

My father in 1926

My father at the age of 30, 1928

My father's Leica

It was during this early time with Herlango that he published the article, *Die Hochtemperaturtrocknung photographischer Schichten* [High Temperature Drying of Photographic Sheets] in the magazine entitled 'Die Photographie

Industrie', Vol. 9, 1927. The radio station RAVAG was founded in 1924 as the first Austrian broadcasting company. The following pages pay tribute to some of his photography and are examples of the themes he lectured on.

Photographie im Dunkeln

DR. ING. OTTO PAPESCH

Vortrag am Dienstag, 3. April, 15,20 Uhr

Die Photographie im Dunkeln oder richtiger gesagt, die Photographie mit infraroten, also für das menschliche Auge unsichtbaren Strahlen, ist eine der interessantesten Errungenschaften der letzten Zeit. Da außer einem speziell sensibilisierten Negativmaterial keinerlei besondere Vorbedingungen nötig sind und die Aufnahmen mit jeder gewöhnlichen Kamera gemacht werden können, werden weite Kreise der Amateur- und Fachphotographie interessiert sein zu erfahren, wieweit das neue Material für ihre Zwecke Verwendung finden kann. Der Vortrag macht sich zur Aufgabe, darüber Aufschluß zu geben.

1. Aufnahme mit gewöhnlicher orthochromatischer Platte
2. Aufnahme auf einer für Infrarot sensibilisierten Platte

Aufn. Dr. Ing. O. Papesch

Was viele Photoliebhaber nicht wissen

Vorsatzlinsen, Gelbscheiben und Aufnahmematerial

HERMANN BRÜHLMEYER

Vortrag am Freitag, 6. April, 15,20 Uhr

Der Vortragende erklärt, wie der Bildausschnitt durch Vorsatzlinsen verändert und wie die Wiedergabe der Tonwerte im Bild durch entsprechende Gelbscheiben und durch das Aufnahmematerial beeinflußt werden kann. Im Besonderen wird auf die Fehlererscheinungen, die bei falschem Gebrauch dieser Hilfsmittel entstehen, aufmerksam gemacht und deren richtige Anwendung besprochen.

3. Aufnahme mit Gelbfilter Nr. 2. — 4. Aufnahme ohne Vorsatzlinse mit Hochverstellung des Objektivs, Brennweite 10,5 cm, Blende 25, Belichtungszeit 45". — 5. Aufnahme mit Vorsatzlinse und mit Hochverstellung des Objektivs, Brennweite 9 cm, Blende 25, Belichtungszeit 30". — 6. Aufnahme mit Vorsatzlinse ohne Abblendung 1:4,5, Brennweite 18 cm, Belichtungszeit 4,5". — 7. Aufnahme mit Vorsatzlinse, Brennweite 18 cm, Blende 25, Belichtungszeit 2½ Minuten.

Abb. 4 bis 7 sind vom selben Standpunkt aus aufgenommen

Aufnahmen H. Brühlmeyer

RADIO-WIEN, Heft 27, Seite 8

RAVAG lecture by Otto Papesch on photographing in the dark

Wintersport-photographie

DR. ING. OTTO PAPESCH

Vortrag am Donnerstag, 7. Jänner, 17.15 Uhr

Die Wintersportphotographie ist ein bisher ziemlich vernachlässigter Zweig der Amateurphotographie. Die Ursache dieser Erscheinung ist aber nicht im Mangel an Interesse bei den Lichtbildnern zu suchen, sondern in der unrichtigen Annahme, daß die Wintersportphotographie mehr oder minder ein Privileg der Fachphotographen und Reporter sei. Der Vortragende will zeigen, worauf es dabei ankommt und wie man auch mit einfachen Kameras gute Sportbilder herstellen kann.

Buntes Leben um uns

(Naturbeobachtungen)

Mit Führung am Sonntag, 17. Jänner 1937

HEINZ SCHEIBENPFLUG

Vortrag am Samstag, 9. Jänner, 16.45 Uhr

Nun ist die Zeit des wirklichen Hochwinters gekommen und hat die Natur einschneidend und entscheidend verändert. War bisher nur die Landschaft der Berge in winterliches Weiß gekleidet, so sind es nun auch Täler und Ebenen oder werden es in Kürze sein. Aber wir haben den Tiefpunkt des Lebensstillstandes überwunden, die Entwicklung geht gerade jetzt, wo uns der Winter, wo uns Frost und Eis erst fühlbar und sichtbar werden, mit Riesenschritten dem Frühling entgegen. Die Knospen an den Bäumen schwellen immer mehr und mehr an und die Triebe der vielen Erstlingsblüher schieben sich langsam der Oberfläche zu, um an den ersten warmen Februartagen auch schon mit ihren Blüten bereit zu sein, ihr kurzes Leben so rasch als möglich emporzutragen und für das Fruchten bereit zu sein!

Jetzt ist die Zeit auch gekommen, die uns besonders tief und gut in die Geheimnisse des stillen und heimlichen Lebens eindringen läßt, denn allerorts finden wir Fährten, Spuren und Zeichen des tierischen Lebens. Ein bißchen Fährtenkunde wollen wir denn auch in unseren Vortrag betreiben.

FÜHRUNG: Am Sonntag, 17. Jänner, findet unter der Leitung des Vortragenden eine Führungsfahrt in den winterlichen Bergwald statt. Wir werden Gelegenheit haben, Leben und Lebensgemeinschaften des Winterwaldes in einer prächtigen Voralpengegend kennen und schauen zu lernen, außerdem werden Burg Feistritz und die niederösterreichische Tropfsteinhöhle, die Hermannshöhle, besichtigt. Fahrt mit Sonderzug und Sonderautobussen Wien—Aspang—Feistritz—Kirchberg am Wechsel—Hermannshöhle—Aspang—Wien. Abfahrt Wien-Aspangbahnhof um 8 Uhr früh. Fahrt und Führung S 8.50. Teilnahme nur gegen Voranmeldung (Aspangbahnhof oder Volksbildungsverein, V., Stöbergasse 11) bis spätestens 14. Jänner möglich!

Turnen

Sendewoche 3. bis 9. Jänner

RADIO-WIEN, Heft 14, Seite 10

RAVAG lecture by Otto Papesch on photographing winter sport activities

Photographie und Kriminalistik

DR. ING. OTTO PAPESCH

Als Seelsorger bei den Bauarbeitern der Glocknerstraße

P. FRANZ STILETZ

WIR LERNEN VOLKSLIEDER

KARL M. KLIER

GESELLSCHAFTSLIED

Seite 7, Heft 20, RADIO-WIEN

RAVAG lecture by Otto Papesch on photography and criminology

Margarete *On Lake Garda*

Winter sport

Puss in a boot

Landscape with portrait

Monument

Portrait: My mother in Wörschach

Sport: rowing

Leisure time

Winter sport

Photographing by night

Experiment: shadows

Spring: View from the house on the Eichelhof down to the Danube and the start of the Danube Canal

As already mentioned, my father worked at Herlango, the photographic establishment of his uncle Ferdinand from 1921 onwards. He firstly worked in the firm's chemical laboratory and later in the department for celloidal paper, barytage and chemical production. He later became head of the photographic plates section.

The production branch of Herlango Pty. Ltd. was cut off from the firm and Ferdinand Hrdliczka founded a new company called Lainer & Hrdliczka with Professor Alexander Lainer. My father assumed the same position there that he had previously held at Herlango Pty. Ltd. and also worked on the production of important types of photographic papers.

My father gave lectures on the radio in the 1930s until the Nazis closed the station. A whole series of subjects concerning photography were covered, including night shots, photographing street scenes, buildings, nature, sports, plants, mountains, ships, leisure time, villages, monuments, landscapes, trips, work, portraits, nudes, still life, infrared photography and criminology.

An article in *Radio Wien*, Number 30, of 20 April 1934, announced that Dr Otto Papesch was to give a lecture on 26 April 1934 on the abnormal reaction of photographic layers, from 4.45 to 4.55 pm.

My father resigned from his position at Lainer & Hrdliczka on 31 March 1938.

It is possible that he took up a position with Wien Film on 1 April 1938. I did not find any relevant documentation concerning this move. However, I did find a note dated 15 July 1945 confirming that my father was employed by Wien Film as technical consultant from 15 August 1941 (that was just one day after he had returned to Vienna from Poland on the grounds of having being afflicted with tuberculosis) until 15 July 1945.

The laboratory at the Herlango firm

My father held a series of lectures on photography during the years 1944/45.

My father with groups of his students

Subjects included the history of cinematography, celluloid, production and processing, production of plates, papers, films, lighting procedures, development, focussing, how a photograph is created, the camera, sensitometry, 100 years of photography and the beginnings of optics. I could not find any further documentation on possible other subjects my father might have lectured on. The articles my father wrote from 1927 onwards for inclusion in the Herlango magazine, *Illustriertes Monatsheft für Amateure* (Illustrated Monthly Magazine for Amateurs), the *Illustierten Wochenschrift der österreichischen Radioverkehrs-AG* (Illustrated Weekly of the Austrian Radio Network Pty. Ltd.) and *Das Photo Magazin* (The Photo Magazine) no longer exist, just the titles. Other titles of his articles include: *Für die Photo-Babys, Photographische Unterrichtsbriefe für Anfänger* (For Photo Babies: Training Letters for Beginners in Photography), *Der Werdegang einer photographischen Platte* (How a Photographic Plate is Developed), *Zum 50. Unterrichtskurs der Herlango AG* (50th Anniversary of the Training Courses at Herlango Pty. Ltd.), *Die Erzeugung photographischer Papiere* (The Production of Photographic Papers), *Aus der Praxis für die Praxis: Gelbschleier* (From Lab to Application: the Yellow Filter), *Wann ist das Negativ ausentwickelt?* (When has the Negative Finished Developing?), *Aufnahme bei Nacht* (Taking Photos at Night), *Die Photoausrüstung des Skiläufers* (The Skier's Photographic Equipment), *Aufnahmen im Frühling* (Taking Photos in Spring), *Über die Wahl des Motivs bei der Landwirtschaftsaufnahme* (About the Choice of Subjects when Photographing Farming Scenes), *Portraits*, *Wintersportphotographie* (Winter Sport Photos), *Mit Faltboot und Kamera* (Underway with a Faltboat and a Camera), *Über den Gebrauch von Vorsatzlinsen* (Usage of an Ancillary Lens), *Abnormale Reaktion der photographischen Schicht* (Abnormal Reaction of the Photographic Layer), *Die Sache mit dem goldenen Schnitt* (The Question of the Golden Mean), *Ruine Aggstein* (The Aggstein Ruin), *Festbeleuchtung der Karlskirche* (Illumination of St Charles Church), *Die Hausfrau am Herd* (Housewife at the Stove), *Spitz a. d. Donau*, *Blüten* (Blossoms), *Winterwald* (Forest in Winter), *Sommerstimmung* (Summer Mood), *Herbststimmung (Bäume)* [Autumn Mood (Trees)], *Architektur u. Räume* (Architecture and Rooms), *Photographie von Pflanzen* (Photographing Plants). The titles of these articles are testimony to the range and diversity of my father's interests when applying his photographic skills.

1929: My Parents Fall in Love and Wed On 6 June 1931

My parents met in 1929 in Mallwitz.

My parents on the ski slopes of Mallwitz, 1929 (with the little card my father attached: "To my dear Ducky in memory of the happy days in Mallwitz, Otti"

The photos show a couple in love, either on ski slopes in winter or going swimming or canoeing in summer. I'm not certain if my parents ever got officially engaged. It was another two years till my mother returned to Vienna from the United States in February 1931. During those two years, my father wrote over 100 letters and postcards to my mother; in other words, at least one or the other every day. In one of them, he asked my mother whether there could be a market for his photos along with articles about sport or Austrian landscapes.

Much of the correspondence between 1929 and 1931 was damaged through humidity and was hardly legible. I didn't find any letters that my mother would have written to my father. My father always wrote most affectionately to my mother. He obviously inherited his love of writing letters from his mother who corresponded with all her relatives and friends on a continuous basis for decades.

In his letter dated 16 July 1930, one can sense how my father's being was affected by his past experiences and how it would later affect my parents' marriage. *In your last letter, you criticised me for being too rational. I make no secret of the fact that I continuously attempt to approach all things rationally. I don't always succeed. However, I can state that I am living my life now; in the past, my life was lived for me! As a result of my reaching this state, many resources such as enthusiasm and enchantment that lead to high-performance levels got washed away. In this way, I am able to manage my life somewhat better. In this way also there is no danger of slipping into the pressure sphere of external influences. Oh my Little One, how my emotions were misused in the past! I have had to struggle hard before being able to reach this small platform which I have already described to you.*

My father's talents were not confined to photography. His historical essay and description of the Wachau, which he included in his letter, are a delight to read. He seems to have even contemplated of writing further articles along these lines as a possible source of future income.

Dürnstein from my Faltboat, July 1930

Schönbühel from my Faltboat, July 1930

My parents were married on 6 June 1931. As I was going through the mountains of documents relating to my father that led to this biography, I found one where it states that he left the Catholic Church on 24 April 1931.

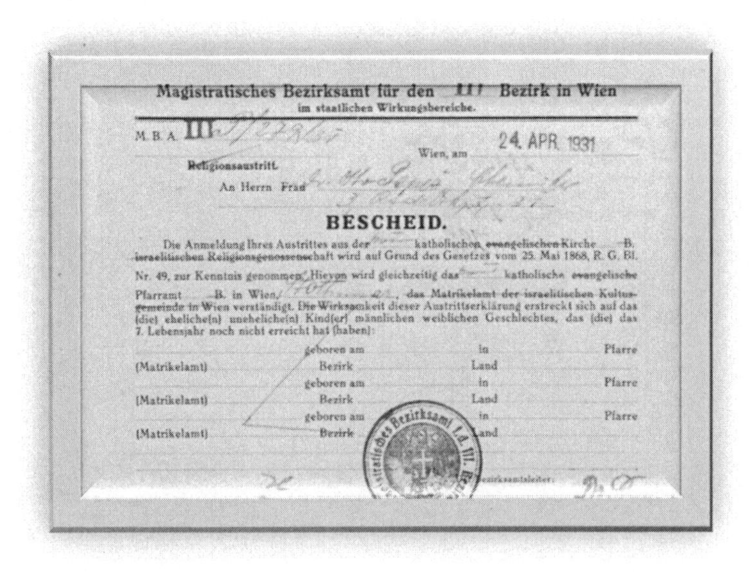

Magistratisches Bezirksamt für den III Bezirk in Wien
im staatlichen Wirkungsbereiche.

M. B. A. III

Wien, am 24. APR. 1931

Religionsaustritt.

An Herrn ~~Frau~~

BESCHEID.

Die Anmeldung Ihres Austrittes aus der katholischen ~~evangelischen~~ Kirche ~~B. israelitischen Religionsgenossenschaft~~ wird auf Grund des Gesetzes vom 25. Mai 1868, R. G. Bl. Nr. 49, zur Kenntnis genommen. Hievon wird gleichzeitig das katholische ~~evangelische~~ Pfarramt ~~B.~~ in Wien, ~~das Matrikelamt der israelitischen Kultusgemeinde in Wien~~ verständigt. ~~Die Wirksamkeit dieser Austrittserklärung erstreckt sich auf das (die) eheliche(n) uneheliche(n) Kind(er) männlichen weiblichen Geschlechtes, das (die) das 7. Lebensjahr noch nicht erreicht hat (haben):~~

geboren am in Pfarre
(Matrikelamt) Bezirk Land
geboren am in Pfarre
(Matrikelamt) Bezirk Land
geboren am in Pfarre
(Matrikelamt) Bezirk Land

Bezirksamtsleiter:

Confirmation that my father withdrew from the Catholic Church on 24 April 1931

The wedding photos show that my parents were married at the registry office and not in church. I never found any photos of a church ceremony.

The wedding photo of my parents, 6 June 1931

My parents shortly after having married

My father must have had a reason for leaving the church just days before his wedding. That would fit what my mother told me that my father was absolutely firm about never having any children. Perhaps it had to do with his experiences during the war. One of the things that was discussed in my father's correspondence with my mother was where to get married and where to settle down. Uncle Vicki had already emigrated to the United States with his fiancée, Mary. My parents chose to settle in Vienna in a flat in Rinößlgasse in the 4th District. In a letter to my mother in early 1931, before she returned to Austria, my father described the layout and furnishings of their flat.

The flat in Rienößlgasse 22/6 in the 4th District

In the living room:

- Piano
- Desk
- Display cabinet
- Inlaid chest
- Round table
- Sofa 1
- Sofa 2

In the dining room:

- Small black table in the corner
- Sofa next to it
- Sideboard
- Table in the middle
- Wardrobe with drawers (under the big picture)
- Fauteuils along the walls
- Sofa

In your bedroom... (Your!!! Bedroom)

- Large wardrobe
- Small wardrobe
- Books
- Card table
- Bed
- Small bedside table

There is no description of the layout and furniture in "his" bedroom. In any case, my parents had separate bedrooms from the very start of their marriage. As it turned out, their marriage was not to be a happy one, almost right from the beginning. Numerous conflicts and intense stress between my parents broke out almost immediately. Shortly before my mother returned from America in November 1931 (there had been an outbreak of typhoid in the Herter family and my mother was called to help with their crisis), my father wrote quite a long letter to her:

I think the world one builds for oneself should be small and secluded and far from external adversities. You will help me with that now, won't you, Moidele? A peaceful home and you and me understanding each other—I think that it is the least one should be allowed to expect from life and marriage. Come, my little rabbit. I long to see you again! We shall understand each other now that the early storm has passed.

My mother spent the first wedding anniversary with her parents'-in-law in Wörschach. My father wrote her a long letter the day after:

Moidi, you wrote me such endearing lines the day after our wedding anniversary. However, your letter confirms to me what I already know and that is that you are often very unhappy. You even mention that you are totally despondent and suffer moments of deep weariness. That seems to be worse than I thought. Moidi, if that is the result of our first year of marriage, then it is best you leave me. What it is that is missing between us is hard to ascertain. Each has their own way of looking at things and is right in their own way. One thing is certain, and I have only become aware of it during this last year, that I have deep-rooted psychological and physical defects. What the causes are and the ensuing results are difficult to ascertain. No one knows whether these things can be put right. One thing is certain, however, it is impossible and doesn't make sense to go on indefinitely if you feel so terribly unhappy as you do in your present circumstances. I can only say again, the average human being must create his own life.

I think it was Tolstoy who wrote that the greatest tragedy that befalls a couple is that of the bed. My father always wrote most tenderly to my mother. He'd call her *Schnurrdiburr* or *Schnurrdibiene*, *Moidele* or *Kleinchen* [little one], or *Haas* [rabbit] or *Ducky*. However, that can be misleading because in the same sentence, he'd write what a good girl she was to have sent a package or written a letter. It is questionable if my father had a romantic streak. He did have a bit of a flirt with his cousins in 1914 and 1915 before he started his military service, but…it would appear that he later became a rather reclusive and most probably emotionally damaged human being after he returned from the front.

My father would often write about how he slept, whether good or bad. He often had sleepless nights and about 6 years later, a Dr Federn was to tell my father that sleepless nights were only a parenthesis in the complex makeup of his character. My mother also suffered from inexplicable states of nervous tension. And last but not least, there was the problem of my mother's mother who was pathologically jealous of her son-in-law. According to my brother, Peter, there was an incident shortly after the end of the war. Our father must have gone out on his bike to the Russian Zone to look for food. Our grandmother apparently yelled out that she hoped the Russians would capture and deport him.

The young couple carried on their relationship as well as they could. I think my father was able to express his emotions more freely in his photographs than in romantic gestures towards my mother. The births of my brother, Peter, and then mine as well as the dire conditions of the 2nd World War brought my parents closer together. My mother would often tell me that she and my father stood back to back once war had broken out.

My parents first lived in Radetzkystraβe 31 in the 3rd District in Vienna, presumably with my grandparents, and later in Rienöβlgasse 22 in the 4th District until they moved to Eichelhofstraβe 2b in Nussdorf with its huge garden.

The house on the Eichelhof was the dream house for both my parents. According to my mother, she, my father and his parents would often go walking up to the Kahlenberg or Leopoldsberg, passing by that house at Number 2b. From there, you could have a most magnificent view of all of Vienna and across the Danube to the Űberschwemmungsgebiet (the flood plain). Conversations would inevitably fall to the house at Number 2b and how wonderful it would be to live there. One day, my grandfather arrived with a newspaper and showed my parents an ad announcing that the property was to be auctioned off. Oh, the excitement that followed! Every time my mother would recall those moments, she would relive her overwhelming feelings.

But now, where to find the money! The house was to cost more than the young couple had in the bank. They sat down to discuss what they could sell to raise some funds. Some objects were hard to let go of. My mother had a terrible time letting go of her favourite bracelet. But it was all worth it in order to acquire their dream home.

The certificate of domicile shows that my parents moved into the house at Eichelhofstraβe 2b in Nussdorf in the 19th District of Vienna on 3 August 1933. Both my mother and my father loved that house that was to create for them so many memories, both happy and tragic.

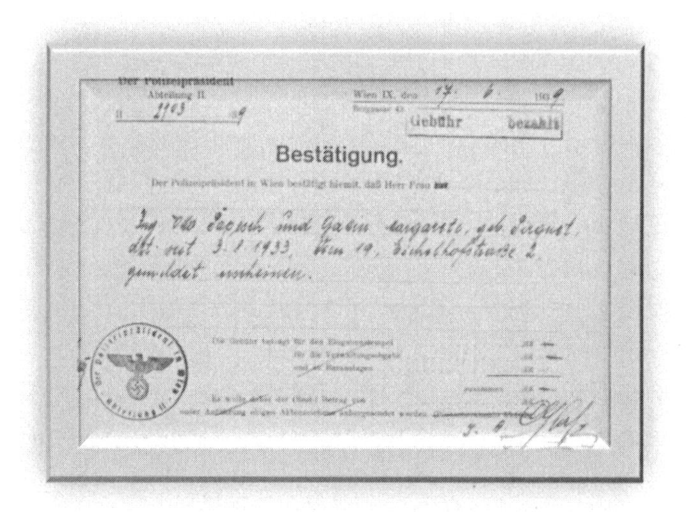

Der Polizeipräsident
Abteilung II.

Wien IX, den 17. 6. 1939

Gebühr bezahlt

Bestätigung.

Der Polizeipräsident in Wien bestätigt hiermit, daß Herr Frau

Certificate of domicile dated 17 June 1939 confirming that my parents moved into the Eichelhof house on 3 August 1933

Left: The House on the Eichelhof (view onto the top terrace from the living room, 1934); Right: View of the house from the Hackhofergasse

The living room on the Eichelhof and the piano my father would often play on

Nussdorf was and still is an adorable little village in the 19th District of Vienna called Döbling. Beethoven lived in innumerable houses and composed his many works there. He directed his 9th Symphony at the parish church and it was also there that my father's great-great-grandmother, Helene Grebner, sang in the choir. Just before reaching Nussdorf, there used to be a market square on the right-hand side of the Heiligenstädterstraβe with flower and fruit and vegetable stalls, a hardware store and pharmacy. The Nüring family ran a *Heurigen* just next to this square where you could sit outside under an immense chestnut tree. There was a stationary shop across the street and on Nussdorf Square itself, there was a butcher, a baker and a restaurant. The Kunz Grocer was a bit further up.

Turning right into Hackhofergasse, almost at the corner, there was the dairy woman's little shop. Further up, Franz Schier had his famous *Heurigen* on the right. Across the street, the Bachofen & Medinge brewery with the Bachofen residence on the other side. Further up again on the right-hand side, you came to the Schickanederschlössel, which Franz Lehár bought in 1932. It is also called the Lehár Schlössel as the composer lived there until 1944. On the left-hand side, you came to the Schottenhof. After that, around the bend, was the beginning of the Eichelhofstraβe with a big door into the wine cellar. Further up was another entrance to the wine cellar, which was turned into an air-raid shelter in 1944.
My parents loved their sport throughout their years together, both in summer as in winter. They'd go skiing or hiking...and my father would always take innumerable photos along the way.

My father's beloved rucksack

He'd also test which film emulsions would be the best for photos taken in freezing conditions, for example. In the summer, my parents would often go swimming in the Danube. They'd take the train upriver, pack their clothes in a swim bubble and swim down to Nussdorf. Or else they'd paddle down the river; they almost went all the way to the Black Sea once. My mother would tell me how they'd camp along the shore of the river and how they'd have to brush their teeth with wine as there was no fresh water around. In 1935, my mother's dear friend, Mac Herter, came to visit with her two sons, Chris Jr and Fred. They all enjoyed their ride on the Danube.

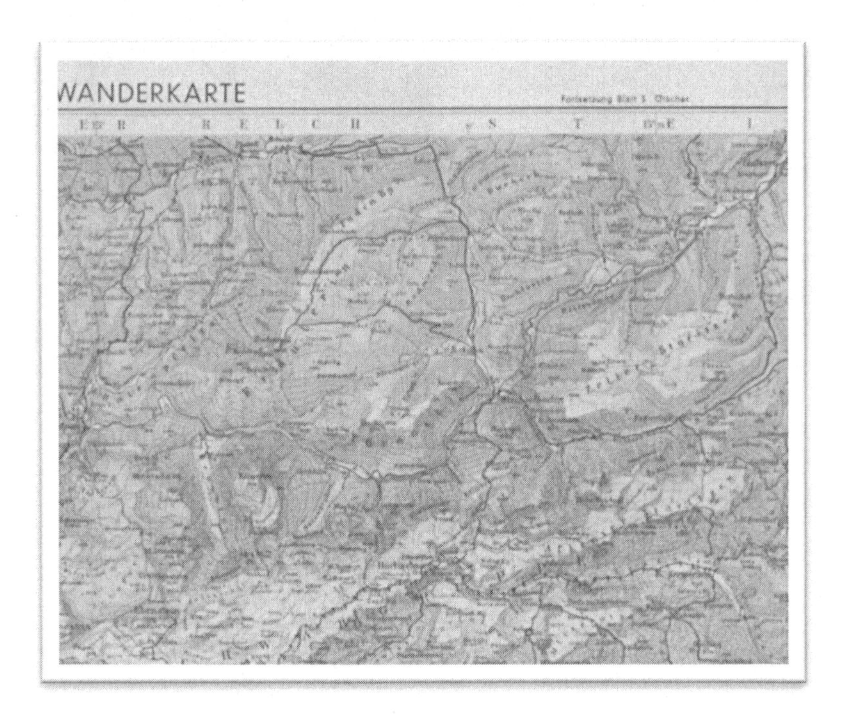

One of my father's many hiking maps

Der Kleingärtner

Von Anton Gipelbauer.

Herbst- oder Frühjahrspflanzung? Di
rbstpflanzung ist vorzuziehen, ausgenommen in sehr kalte
r nassen Lagen. Ferner werden alle empfindlichere
lanzen im Frühjahr gesetzt. Für Stauden (Perennen) i
beste Pflanzzeit September-Oktober. Späteres Pflanze
nnte bewirken, daß die Pflanzen vom Frost aus der Erd
hoben werden. Dagegen kann man sich aber durch Auflege
n Mist, Laub oder Torfstreu schützen. Bäume un
räucher werden im Oktober-November gepflanzt. Pfirsi
t im Frühjahr. Hochstammrosen werden ebenfalls besser i
ühjahr gepflanzt. Niedere Rosen werden bei der Herbs
anzung angehäufelt und die Erde wird zwischen de
lanzen mit oben angegebenem Material abgedeckt. Wei
ben können auch im Herbst gepflanzt werden. Da de
benverkauf in den Rebschulen erst im Frühjahr beginnt, f
rd allgemein im April gepflanzt. Bei Herbstpflanzung wir
Rebe überhäufelt (im Frühjahr allerdings auch, doch zum
utz gegen zu starke Besonnung). Blumenzwiebeln
rden im Oktober-November in den Boden gesteckt.

Schnittlauch und Petersiliengrün. Schnitt
chpflanzen werden im Herbst in Töpfe gesetzt und in Inter
len von zwei bis vier Wochen zum Antreiben in die Küche
s Fenster) gestellt. Nach acht bis vierzehn Tagen kan
n das erstemal geschnitten werden. Nach vier- bis fünf
ligem Schnitt werden neue Pflanzen genommen. Aehnlich
es bei der Petersilie. Die Wurzeln werden in entsprechend
e Töpfe gesetzt (vier bis fünf Stück zusammen) und eben
s in die Küche gestellt. Hat man mehrere solche Töpfe vor
eitet, so kann man den ganzen Winter grüne Blätter haben.
t gießen.

Herbstarbeiten. Unter den Bäumen und zwischen
Sträuchern umstechen, beziehungsweise vorher düngen.
Obstbäume sollen nach dem Laubfall mit Obstbaum-
bolineum oder Bol K gegen alle Arten von Blatt- und
ildläusen, gegen Raupen und dergleichen gespritzt werden.
äter haben sich die Schädlinge schon zu sehr eingewintert,
daß die Spritzwirkung weit ungünstiger ist. Es sei jedoch
drücklich vermerkt, daß Obstbaumkarbolineum und Bol K
r tierische, nicht aber pilzliche Schädlinge ver-
ten. Gegen die Rostpilze wird knapp vor dem Knospen-
bruch mit einer Kupferkalklösung und gegen die Mehltau-
en mit einer Schwefellösung gespritzt. Wichtig ist es, bei
Apfelbäumen bei Blutlaus den Wurzelhals
zulegen und bei eventuellem Befall desselben mit den an-
ebenen Spritzmitteln zu pinseln oder Kalk zu streuen.
sundes Laub wird eingestochen, falls es nicht für andre
cke verwendet wird. Krankes Laub ist zu vernichten. Der
en wird mit kurzem Mist überstreut. Der Gartenkies ist
uräumen und in einer Ecke des Gartens auf Haufen zu
ren, um im Frühjahr wieder aufgebracht zu werden. Nach
Laubfall sind die Bäume auszulichten (nicht zurück-
chneiden). Der Rückschnitt erfolgt bei den Obstbäumen
im Frühjahr. Alle Arten Nachpflanzungen sind durch-
führen. Im Gemüsegarten ist der Endiviensalat zu über-
en. Kann gegen den ersten Frost auch mit Stroh geschützt
den. Alle freien Beete grobschollig umstechen (vorher
gen). Rigolarbeiten bei genügender Bodenfeuchte vor-
men, da dann die Arbeit leichter ist.

Neue Art des Obstbaues. Diese sieht vor, daß
ährige Okulanten auf Paradies- oder Quittenunterlagen
pfel oder Birnen) oder eventuell zurückgebliebene senkrechte
chon so eng zusammengepflanzt werden wie Weinreben,
daß die ganze Pflanzung wie ein Weingarten aussieht.
es Bäumchen bekommt einen Rebenpflock. Die Bäumchen
den durch späten Schnitt, durch eventuelles Abstechen der
rzeln und vor allem durch die schwach wachsende Unterlage
Kurztriebigkeit und damit zur frühzeitigen Fruchtbarkeit
anlaßt und sollen sich innerhalb 10 bis 15 Jahren zu
tragen. In der Gartenbauschule des Fortbildungsschul-
s für Wien in Kagran wurden in diesem Jahre auf einer
che von 100 Quadratmeter 1800 gut entwickelte Früchte

Für scharfe Denker.

Aufgabe 68: „Ermüdung."

Aufgabe 67: „Die beiden Wilderer." — Auflösung.

Der Kleingärtner

Von Anton Eichelbauer.

Newspaper articles about gardening

My parents' love of nature could also be seen in the garden on the Eichelhof. My father planted a variety of fruit trees on the terraces. He planted six walnut trees at the very bottom, then four apricot trees on the next level up and cherry, plum, apple and peach trees on the upper levels. He went about it methodically, cutting out relevant newspaper articles of particular interest.

Because my father worked in a darkroom for most of the day, he was particularly keen to get out into the garden once back at home. My mother told the story that as soon as he'd come in the front door, there would be a trail of first a jacket on the floor, then a shirt, then trousers and lastly shoes and socks. He'd put on his old clothes and shoot off outside. On his days off, he'd go down into the village to purchase whatever he needed. There was another fellow further up the hill who was just as keen a gardener and they made a bet who wore the shabbiest garden 'outfits'. One day, so the story goes, my father came home yelling at the top of his voice, "I've won, I've won!" Apparently, an old lady went up to him in the village and put 10 Schillings into his hand, saying, "Here you are, you poor man."

Left: The garden with steps up from below; Right: The upper terrace and the wall from where Frau Max called down

World War II: My Father is Once Again Sent to the Front

My father aged 40, 1938

Magistrat der Stadt Wien
Magistrats-Abteilung 61, Bevölkerungswesen

M.-Abt. 61 – 27748

Zum Amtsgebrauch für

S 1.– Verwaltungsabgabe entrichtet.

Wien, am

Auszug aus der Heimatrolle

Vom Magistrat der Stadt Wien wird bestätigt, daß

Beruf: Stand:

geboren am in

pol. Bezirk: Land:

am*) 13. 3. 1938 das

Heimatrecht in Wien

besessen hat.

Der Bürgermeister
I. A.:

*) Zum Nachweis der [illegible] gemäß § 1 des [illegible] vom [illegible] 1945, [illegible] ist u. a. der Besitz des Heimatrechtes am 13. III. 1938 erforderlich.
Die [illegible] eines nach dem 30. VI. 1939 [illegible] ist [illegible], weil mit diesem Tage das Heimatrecht abgeschafft wurde.

My father's citizenship certificate dated 13 March 1938

My father once again in uniform, 1938

Dark clouds of the Second World War were gathering on the horizon, however. The medical discharge report of my father indicates that he was called up into the German Army as reserve lieutenant on 8 August 1938. My brother wasn't even a month old. I'm not certain exactly when, but trucks were to carry the army to the Polish front at the end of August 1939. The destination was somewhere in the vicinity of Breslau, some 500 or 600 kilometres from Vienna.

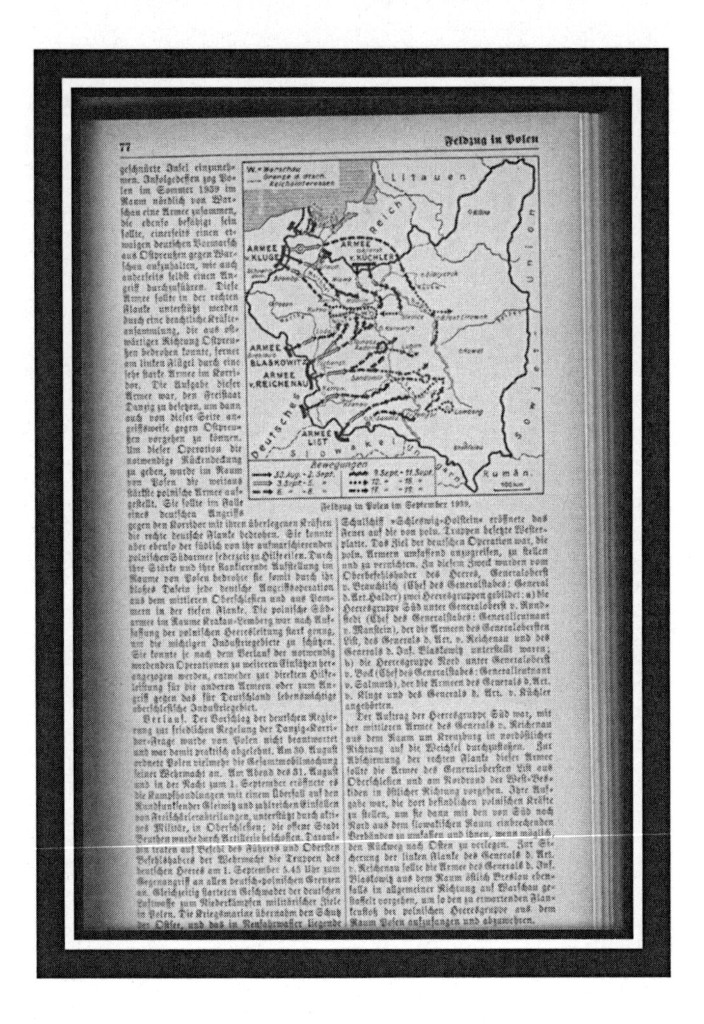

77 Feldzug in Polen

gezeichnete Insel einzunehmen. Infolgedessen zog Polen im Sommer 1939 im Raum nördlich von Warschau eine Armee zusammen, die ebenso befähigt sein sollte, einerseits einen etwaigen deutschen Vormarsch aus Ostpreußen gegen Warschau aufzuhalten, wie auch andererseits selbst einen Angriff durchzuführen. Diese Armee sollte in der rechten Flanke unterstützt werden durch eine beträchtliche Kräfteansammlung, die aus ostwärtiger Richtung Ostpreußen bedrohen konnte, ferner am linken Flügel durch eine sehr starke Armee im Korridor. Die Aufgabe dieser Armee war, den Freistaat Danzig zu besetzen, um dann auch von dieser Seite angriffsweise gegen Ostpreußen vorgehen zu können. Um dieser Operation die notwendige Rückendeckung zu geben, wurde im Raum von Posen die weitaus stärkste polnische Armee aufgestellt. Sie sollte im Falle eines deutschen Angriffs gegen den Korridor mit ihren überlegenen Kräften die rechte deutsche Flanke bedrohen. Sie konnte aber ebenso der südlich von ihr aufmarschierenden polnischen Südarmee jederzeit zu Hilfe eilen. Durch ihre Stärke und ihre flankierende Aufstellung im Raume von Posen bedrohte sie somit durch ihr bloßes Dasein jede deutsche Angriffsoperation aus dem mittleren Oberschlesien und aus Pommern in der tiefen Flanke. Die polnische Südarmee im Raume Krakau-Lemberg war nach Auffassung der polnischen Heeresleitung stark genug, um die wichtigen Industriegebiete zu schützen. Sie konnte je nach dem Verlauf der notwendig werdenden Operationen zu weiteren Einsätzen herangezogen werden, entweder zur direkten Hilfeleistung für die anderen Armeen oder zum Angriff gegen das für Deutschland lebenswichtige oberschlesische Industriegebiet.

Verlauf. Der Vorschlag der deutschen Regierung zur friedlichen Regelung der Danzig-Korridor-Frage wurde von Polen nicht beantwortet und war damit praktisch abgelehnt. Am 30. August ordnete Polen vielmehr die Gesamtmobilmachung seiner Wehrmacht an. Am Abend des 31. August und in der Nacht zum 1. September eröffnete es die Kampfhandlungen mit einem Überfall auf den Rundfunksender Gleiwitz und zahlreichen Einfällen von Freischärlerabteilungen, unterstützt durch aktives Militär, in Oberschlesien; die offene Stadt Beuthen wurde durch Artillerie beschossen. Daraufhin traten auf Befehl des Führers und Obersten Befehlshabers der Wehrmacht die Truppen des deutschen Heeres am 1. September 5.45 Uhr zum Gegenangriff an allen deutsch-polnischen Grenzen an. Gleichzeitig starteten Geschwader der deutschen Luftwaffe zum Niederkämpfen militärischer Ziele in Polen. Die Kriegsmarine übernahm den Schutz der Ostsee, und das in Neufahrwasser liegende Schulschiff »Schleswig-Holstein« eröffnete das Feuer auf die von poln. Truppen besetzte Westerplatte. Das Ziel der deutschen Operationen war, die poln. Armeen umfassend anzugreifen, zu stellen und zu vernichten. Zu diesem Zweck wurden vom Oberbefehlshaber des Heeres, Generaloberst v. Brauchitsch (Chef des Generalstabes: General d. Art. Halder) zwei Heeresgruppen gebildet: a) die Heeresgruppe Süd unter Generaloberst v. Rundstedt (Chef des Generalstabes: Generalleutnant v. Manstein), der die Armeen des Generalobersten List, des Generals d. Art. v. Reichenau und des Generals d. Inf. Blaskowitz unterstellt waren; b) die Heeresgruppe Nord unter Generaloberst v. Bock (Chef des Generalstabes: Generalleutnant v. Salmuth), der die Armeen des Generals d. Art. v. Kluge und des Generals d. Art. v. Küchler angehörten.

Der Auftrag der Heeresgruppe Süd war, mit der mittleren Armee des Generals v. Reichenau aus dem Raum um Kreuzburg in nordöstlicher Richtung auf die Weichsel durchzustoßen. Zur Abschirmung der rechten Flanke dieser Armee sollte die Armee des Generalobersten List aus Oberschlesien und am Nordrand der West-Beskiden in östlicher Richtung vorgehen. Ihre Aufgabe war, die dort befindlichen polnischen Kräfte zu stellen, um sie dann mit den von Süd nach Nord aus dem slowakischen Raum einbrechenden Verbänden zu umfassen und ihnen, wenn möglich, den Rückweg nach Osten zu verlegen. Zur Sicherung der linken Flanke des Generals d. Art. v. Reichenau sollte die Armee des Generals d. Inf. Blaskowitz aus dem Raum östlich Breslau ebenfalls in allgemeiner Richtung auf Warschau gestaffelt vorgehen, um so den zu erwartenden Flankenstoß der polnischen Heeresgruppe aus dem Raum Posen aufzufangen und abzuwehren.

Feldzug in Polen im September 1939.

Map of the invasion of Poland, 1 September 1939. Excerpt from the "Taschen-Brockhaus zum Zeitgeschehen, 1940," page 77

The attack on Poland and specifically Wieluń and nearby towns was carried out on 1 September 1939 with 1.5 million soldiers, 2,400 tanks and 2,500 aeroplanes. It had been a particularly hot summer and the roads were covered in dust or in mud. My mother was always of the opinion that my father's tuberculosis developed in the early years of the war. My father, the professional photographer that he was, must have taken quite a number of rolls of film with him because there exists a photo album of 141 shots from the convoy and his time in Poland (the entire album is featured in the Appendix.) My father wrote captions for each shot, some funny, some of military interest and some rather bleak.

Excerpts from my father's photo album. "On the road to Poland, 1939. The roads were either covered in dust or cars literally sank in the mud"

Excerpts from my father's photo album. Top: The division just before Krakow; Bottom: The head chancery

Excerpts from my father's photo album: Top: The hungry one;
Bottom: Expert assessment

Excerpts from my father's photo album: Top: Two single files; Bottom: Gushing waters in the weir

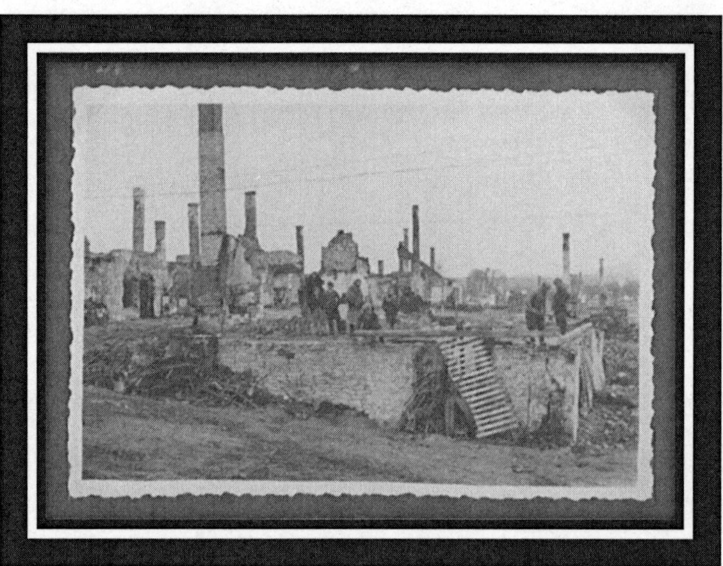

Excerpts from my father's photo album: Top: Endless columns of prisoners;
Bottom: Sorrowful homecoming

Excerpts from my father's photo album: Crossover into Russian territory

Excerpts from my father's photo album: The big pontoon bridge across the Vistula River

Excerpts from my father's photo album: The Ghetto of Tarlow

Excerpts from my father's photo album: The march into Warsaw

No photos exist after they marched into Warsaw. Perhaps my father ran out of rolls of film or taking photos was forbidden. My father was discharged on 14 August 1941 due to tuberculosis in the upper lobes of both lungs.

First Lieutenant Otto Papesch with his camera

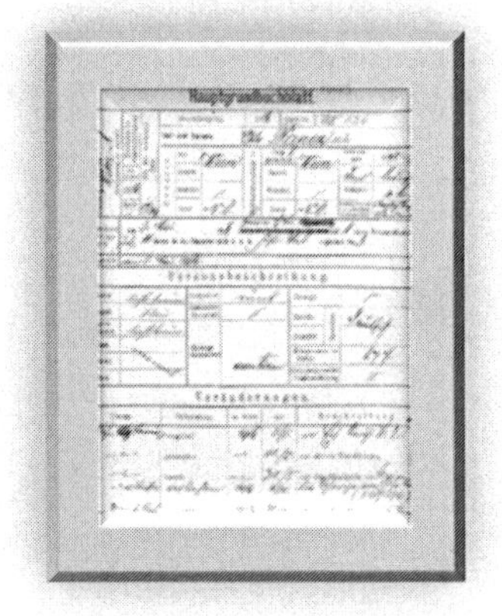
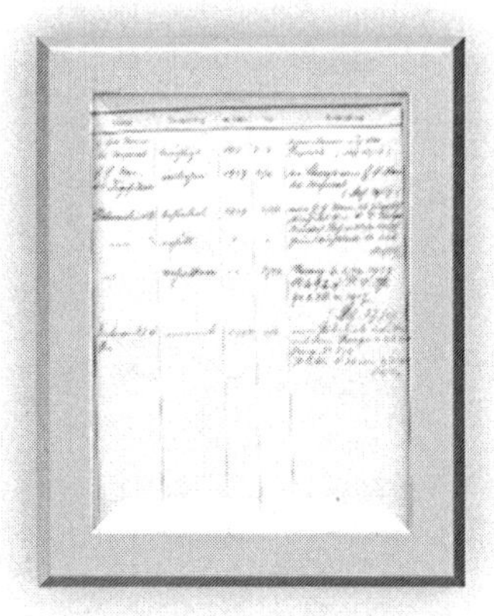

Otto Papesch: Main military register, pages 126/1 and 126/2

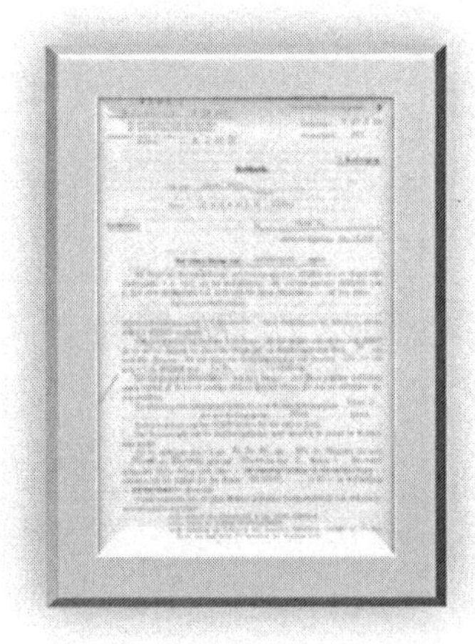

Document dated 20 August 1941, pages 1 and 2, identifying injury

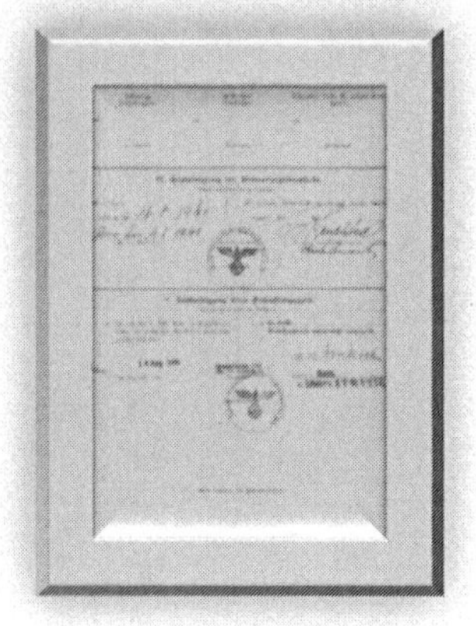

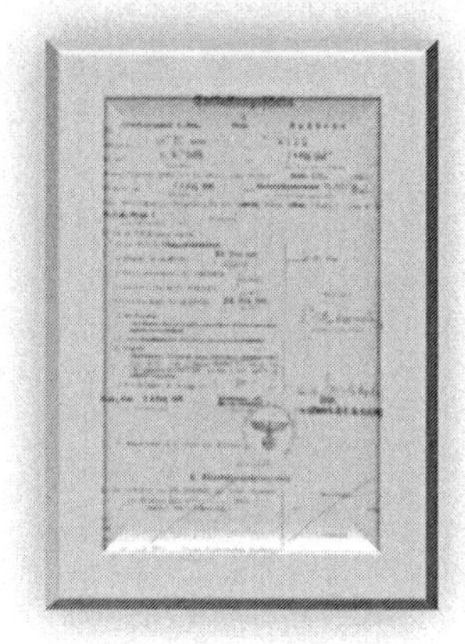

Military discharge certificate dated 14 August 1941, pages 1 and 2

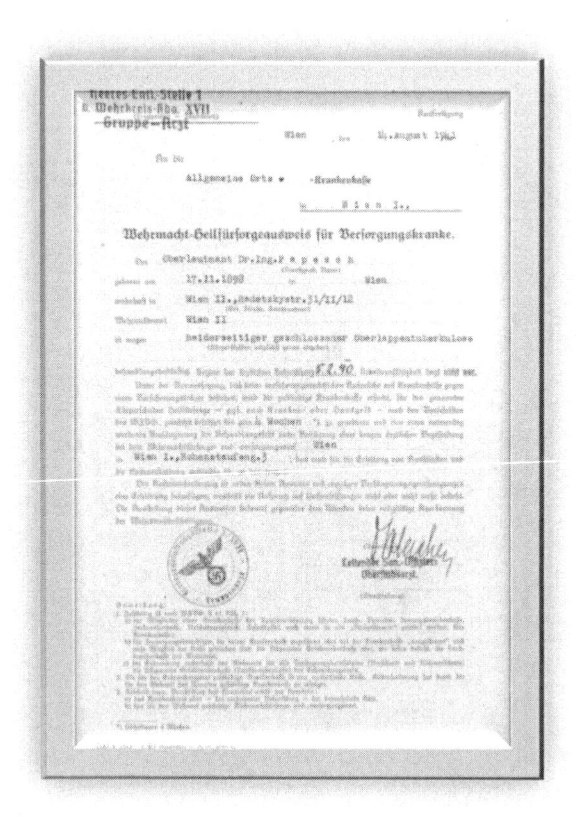

Heeres Entl. Stelle 1
d. Wehrkreis-Kdo. XVII
Gruppe–Arzt

Wien, den 14. August 1941

An die

Allgemeine Orts- Krankenkasse

in Wien I.,

Wehrmacht-Heilfürsorgeausweis für Versorgungskranke.

Oberleutnant Dr.Ing. P a p e s c h

geboren am 17.11.1898 in Wien

wohnhaft in Wien II., Radetzkystr. 31/II/12

Wien II

beiderseitiger geschlossener Oberlappentuberkulose

Wien I., Hohenstaufeng. 3

Otto Papesch: military welfare certificate dated 14 August 1941

Additions to the Family: Otto, the Family Man

Tensions between my parents surfaced on a regular basis, especially in what concerned having children. My mother's yearning to have children seemed to get more and more acute as years went by. Breeding dogs will have offered a bit of a substitute until that was no longer sufficient. The photos of my mother with her Sealyham Terriers (taken by my father, of course) are touching but my personal feeling is that my mother would have preferred carrying human babies around rather than pups, no matter how adorable they might have been.

My mother with her Sealyham Terrier pups

My mother with her favourite dog, Maffy

My father wrote to my mother on 13 November 1937, *Things will get better between us and you will get your little bub that you so desire.*

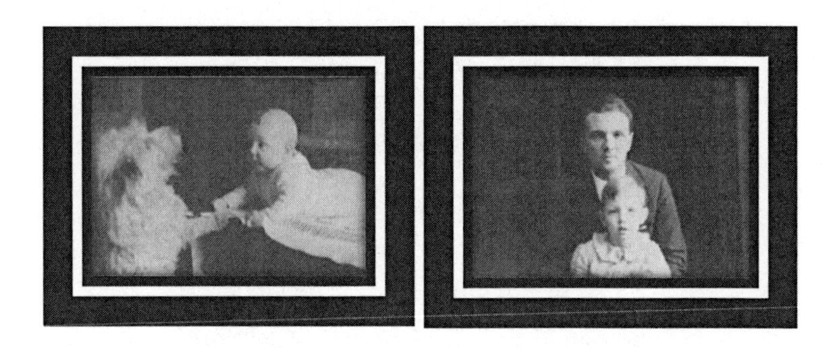

And so my brother was born on 19 July 1938 and my father was ecstatic, much to his own surprise. In what concerns children, it is clear that my father changed his mind once we were born. Firstly, there was his son, Peter, who was born on 19 July 1938 and then, after his return in 1941 from Poland, I was born on 29 April 1943. The charming photos my father took of us speak more than what words could describe. They show that family life was very important to him.

My ecstatic mother with her 3-year-old son Peter after the return of my father from Poland in 1941

My father with his son, Peter, 1941

My father with me, 1943

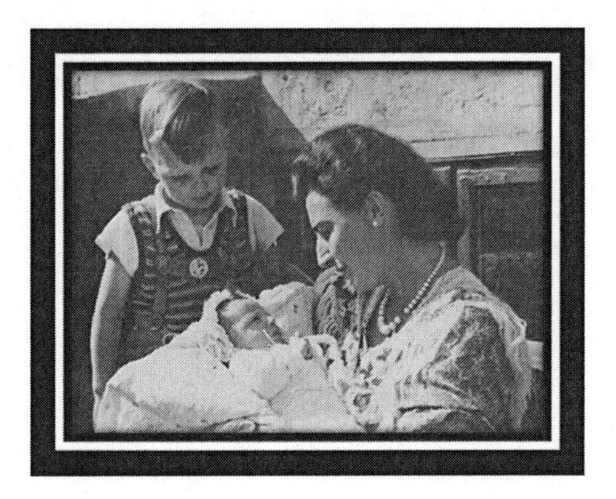

My mother with Peter and me, 1943

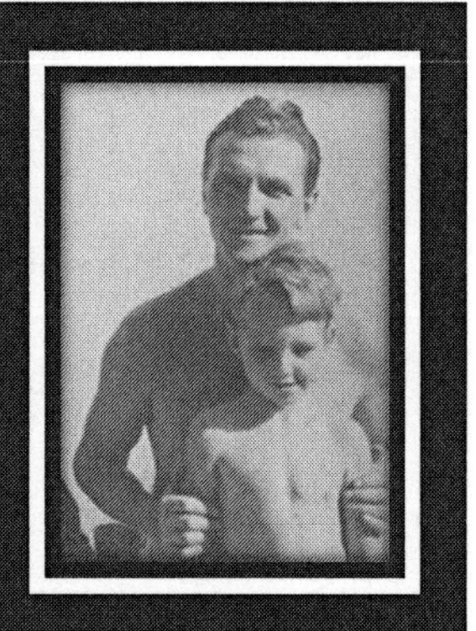

My father with his son, Peter

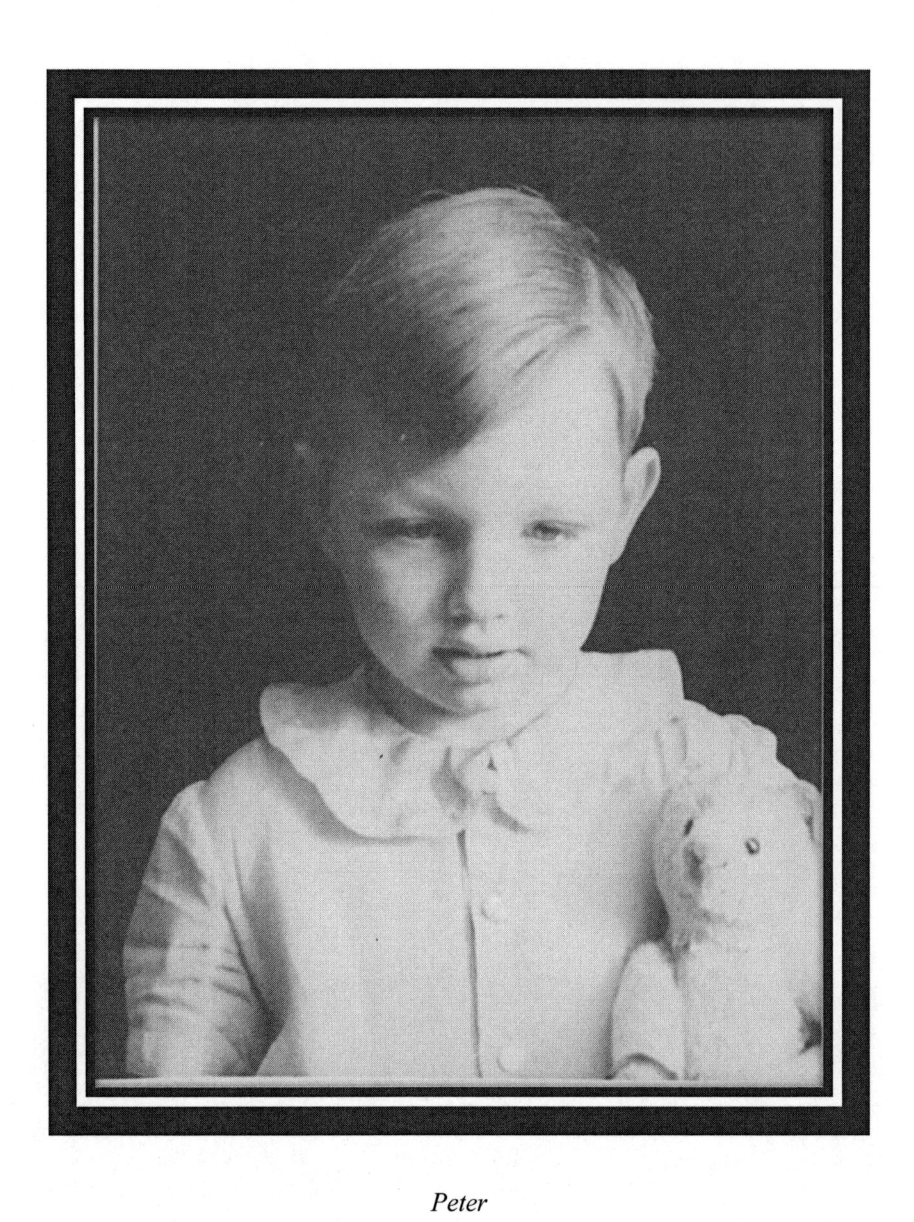

Peter

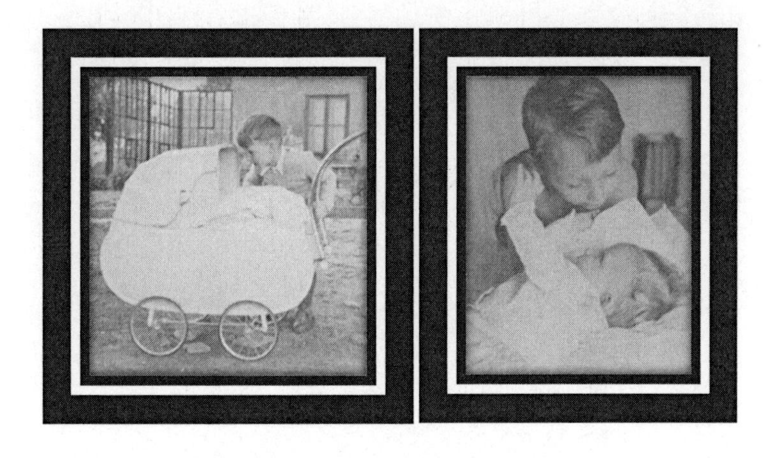

Peter with his little sister

Brother and sister, 1945

My mother beaming with her two children

My mother often told me how deeply attached my father was to his parents. One can sense his deep affection for them from the photos of him with his father and mother.

My father (Leica under his arm) with his father, Ottokar, 1938

My father with his mother, whom he loved most dearly

My father with his dad on one of their hiking tours

He seemed to have been close to his brother, Viktor, in their younger years. In his correspondence from Budapest, as for example on 15 May 1916, he wrote at the end *Greeting to Mops*. Once Vicki had emigrated to the United States it seems that this relationship was broken off as there is nothing in the documents that would indicate that the brothers wrote to each other much. However, my father did think of Vicki's son, Roger, when indicating in his will who was to receive his stamp collection. Roger was to receive the overseas stamps, but only if he should be at all interested, which my father thought was unlikely.

My father in uniform, 1916, and a soldier again in 1939. In between, the man who loved nature.

The experience of war produced fissures in the lives of everyone. My mother would often say that every man who returned from war had a crack somewhere in his psyche. As already mentioned, my father didn't want to put any children into the world for a long time. It is difficult to imagine nowadays with what means a pregnancy was to be avoided back then. Whatever preventative measures they were must have had an effect on the intimacy or perhaps lack thereof between my parents.

My father was apparently very strict and very frugal with money. My mother would often tell me that she had to add to the household budget from her own funds. My father was also very strict in his method of parenting. My brother once told me how very hard my father had been towards him. According to Peter, we had an au-pair named Margit in 1946. My mother had a diamond ring that disappeared one day. Margit was accused of having stolen it. She denied it and our tenant, Mr Skrehunetz, took her side saying that he had seen Peter take the ring. And so, the young boy was accused of the theft and as punishment, locked into the cold and dark coal cellar for 8 hours. My brother can remember this episode to this day and the unpleasant taste in his mouth that it left.

Did such methods come from the military training my father received or was it part of the times when a child had no say? My mother would often mention that I would have had a much stricter upbringing had my father lived. She was much more lenient.

My Father's Last Years: 1945 to 1947

I'm not certain at exactly what day my grandparents were bombed out. Possibly during the air raids the Russians carried out on Vienna's 3rd, "Landstraβe" District on 17 October and on 3, 5 and 6 November 1944. The housing shortage also meant that a given number of people had to live in a large house such as ours. I don't know when that legislation was introduced but my grandparents lived in the upper storey in the room facing east. My maternal grandmother also lived with us as did one of her cousins. Mr Skrehunetz occupied the large room upstairs facing north. My brother and I slept in the children's room downstairs and my mother in the little room next door. Only the kitchen was heated in the cold months. If you think that we were all confined to that room of about $20m^2$, it isn't hard to imagine that things could get quite hot—and not because of the cooking.

My father stayed in Hotel Surböck in Mariazell for a while in January 1944, either for a holiday or most likely to get some rest. He wrote to my mother, *I suddenly have this aversion against sugar and sweets. I should stop eating meals because they disgust me. I have never experienced anything like it ever before. I have an urge of pouring salt into my soup and on all the other dishes. I don't do it because it can't be good. Is this a change from sweet to sour, is it old age creeping in, I don't know... I can't wait to go through with Dr Sattler's examination. If he can't prescribe a draconian cure for me, I'll drop everything. It is unlikely that I will be allowed to take another holiday like this for years. I feel neither rested nor refreshed, quite the contrary. I feel tired and listless and very little and ugly.*

The Red Army had reached Vienna at the beginning of April 1944 or possibly already at the end of March. It reached Baden and Preβburg on 2 April. The battle went on north of the Danube till 18 April until the Russians had captured the area around St Pölten.

According to Leopold Grulich, Vienna was subjected to between 53 and 57 bombardments from 12 April 1944 to 23 March 1945. The 19th District, Döbling, was hit 20 times during that period:

16 July 1944
10 September 1944
17 October 1944
5, 6, 15 and 18 November 1944
2, 3, 18 and 26 December 1944
15 January 1945
7 and 20 February 1945
12, 13, 15, 19, 21 and 22 March 1945

Marshall Tolbuchin declared that the battle for Vienna ended on 13 April 1945.

My mother told my brother and me that the house on the Eichelhof was hit by two bombs and 18 grenades. There was a huge hole in the garden, damage to brickwork and a big gap in the wall of the bathroom where you could see straight through onto the terrace below. We lived with the damage for many years after the war and my father's death until my mother was able to have the house repaired in 1952.

Because the house on the Eichelhof had such an extensive view of Vienna and the surrounding regions, the Russians confiscated it and turned it into a radio station. I don't know when exactly that happened, but frantic preparations were made in order to hide as much as possible from pilfering Russians. According to my mother, my father spent day and night digging in the garden and hiding the family's valuables—heavy work for someone with my father's condition that would have warranted continuous rest. The population also suffered from famine. My father is said to have often taken his camera and cycled out into the countryside in order to take portraits of the farmers in return for a sack of potatoes.

We had to move into the air-raid shelter at the bottom of Eichelhofstraβe once the Russians had taken over the house. We were housed there with other families like in a box of sardines. Our neighbour had a 14-year-old daughter named Inge. They were very concerned for her because the Russians were known to rape the women and young girls. My mother smeared ash all over herself in order to appear sick and so she was never molested. However, the Russians sought 14-year-old Inge. Before one of the inspections, my father hid her in the chimney, blowing ash everywhere. The Russians pointed their flashlights up and down the brick walls but thankfully didn't see her.

I was crawling at the time and apparently spent all my energies climbing up the steps in an attempt to get out. I can't remember any of it but the living conditions in that hole must have been shocking. All this must have again contributed to the stress factor my father was submitted to instead of the peace and quiet that he needed.

I'm not certain when we moved back into the house. Everything had to be lugged up the hill again and other things dug up in the garden—all hard physical work. There was only my father who could do all that work. My grandfather was already 77 years old and my brother was only 7. Mr Skrehunetz was never home till very late at night and so couldn't be of much help.

My father lived with us in the house till the beginning of May 1946 when he was interned in the sanatorium in Grimmenstein for a period of rest. According to the postcard to his cousin, Trudl Hoffman, he stayed there for five months till the end of September. The date on the postcard is 27 August but it was never sent off.

My grandparents stayed with my father for the entire period. There is an ambiguous tone to the content of my grandmother's postcard to her niece. Her words were full of hope, but my grandfather's had something sombre about them. As I mentioned, this postcard was never sent off.

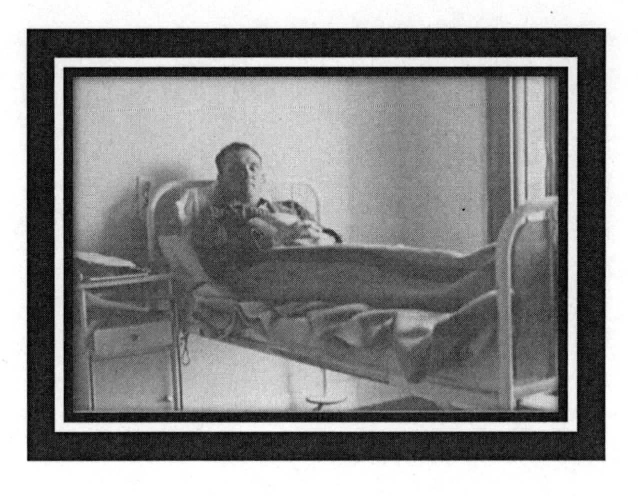

My father at the sanatorium in Grimmenstein

Liebe Trude! Grimmenstein Hochegg 27. Aug.
Versuche ob Dich unsere Grüße erreichen.
Otto ist seit Anfang Mai hier in der Lungenheil-
stätte soll noch bis Ende September bleiben u.
wir bleiben auch so lange. Es ist herrliche Wald-
gegend. Wie geht es Dir, Deinem Gatten und
Peter? Vikis sandten 10 Photos von ihrem kleinen
Eigenheim, mehr außerhalb der Stadt. Kommt
Dein Mann nie nach Chicago? Sollte sie besu-
chen. 7926 Long Ave Morton Grove Chicago.
Es hofft Dich wohlauf u. grüßt Dich u. Deine Männer
vielmals Deine Tante Rit[illegible]

Bin auf einige Zeit hier zur Erholung, und freue mich die
Eltern hier zu haben. Hoffe Euch wohlauf. Herzliche Grüße [illegible]

Otto ist hier im Roten Kreuz, er sieht sehr gut aus
hat eine leichte Lungensache nach den Strapazen.
Herzlichste Grüße an Euch! [illegible]

Franz Schneidhofer, Fotograf, Neunkirchen, N.-Donau 1940

Herrn u. Frau
Werner Hofmann
Villa Road 35
Larchmont
New York U.S.A

Kopie der Originalplatte

Postcard from Grimmenstein with a view of the sanatorium, August 1946

Dear Trude!

I hope this postcard will reach you. Otto is in this sanatorium for tuberculosis patients since the beginning of May and will stay here till the end of September. We will be staying with him for the entire time. It is a beautiful region with surrounding forests. How are you, your husband and Peter? Vicki sent 10 photos of their little house outside of town. Does your husband ever get to Chicago? He should look them up. 7926 Long Ave, Morton Grove, Chicago. I hope you are well and I send you and your men my best regards,

Your Aunt Ritschl.

I'm here for a bit of a rest. I'm happy to have my parents here. I hope you are well.

Best regards, Otto.

Otto is here at the Red Cross. He's looking well, has got a slight condition with his lungs after all the stress.

Best regards to you all, Uncle Otto.

I don't know when my father returned to Vienna and whether he was immediately put into the Lainz Sanatorium, but it must have been shortly after leaving Grimmenstein. I didn't find any documents or medical reports from this time.

As already mentioned, my grandparents stayed with my father for the entire time of his stay there. He was very close to his parents and that can be seen in the many photos of them together and also from the many letters and postcards he wrote to them: *Dearest parents*, *Dearest Mama*, *Dear Daddy*, *My dear little dad…*

There is an entry in his diary of 1917 in which he wrote how concerned he was for his father who had to go for a medical examination. He was most concerned back then and in his will, he was adamant about making sure his parents would be looked after once he had passed away.

My mother left Vienna for the United States in October 1946 in the hope of obtaining streptomycin. Tuberculosis was already being treated there with this antibacterial drug. That would indicate that my father's condition didn't improve at all during his stay in Grimmenstein. I only remember that my mother drove off on a cold autumn day. It was dark already as she stepped into a jeep like the one in the movie *The Third Man*, down on the Heiligenstädterstraβe. My grandparents, Peter and I (with me screeching and howling at the top of my voice) had gone down with her. I remember my mother wore a dark brown fur jacket.

According to my mother, my father was not on the Eichelhof for Christmas 1946 and was never to return there. She was in the States at the time. In other words, he must have been in a hospital from the beginning of May 1946 to the end of April 1947. Eleven long months without getting better or being healed. It fills me with dread when I think what it must have been like for my father lying in bed day after day and night after night, staring death in the face at every moment.

It's eerie what he wrote in his diary back in 1917: *This constant vicinity with death can put you into a bleak mood.*

Streptomycin was being tested in England at the time and apparently in Scandinavia also. My father was never able to receive treatment with that drug. But the life of a collaborator of mine, with whom I worked at FAO in later years, was able to be saved. He was but a toddler in 1946 and was diagnosed with tuberculous meningitis and was near death. He and other children were part of an experiment with this drug and were cured. Streptomycin wasn't available in Vienna till later. 2,000 people succumbed to tuberculosis in Vienna in 1947.

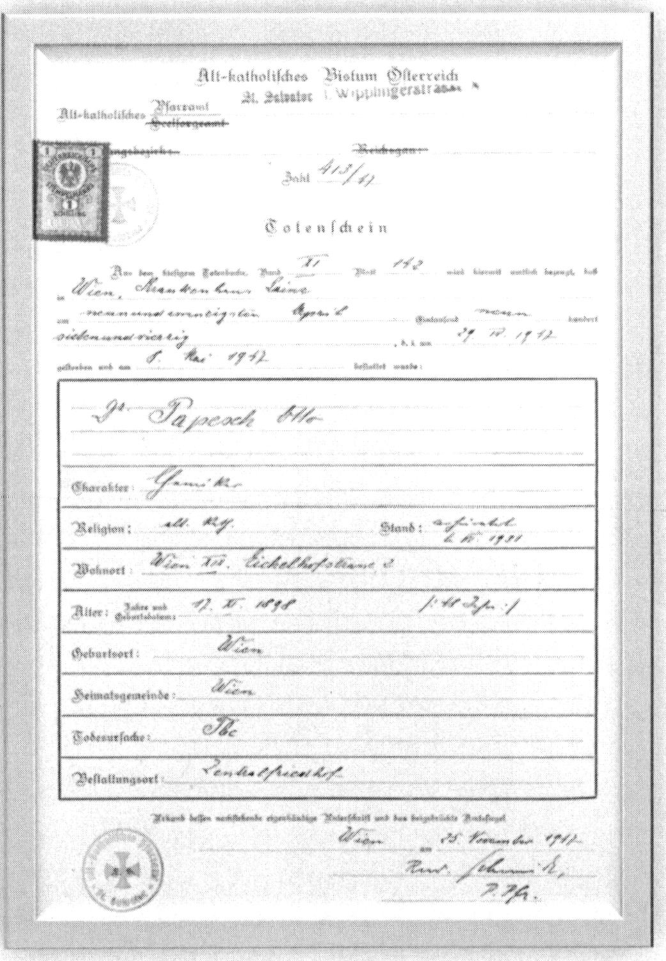

Alt-katholisches Bistum Österreich
St. Salvator I. Wipplingerstrasse

Alt-katholisches Pfarramt ~~Seelsorgeamt~~

Zahl 413/47

Totenschein

Aus dem hiesigen Totenbuche, Band XI Blatt 142 wird hiermit amtlich bezeugt, daß

in Wien, ...

am ... April ... Eintausend neun hundert

siebenundvierzig, d. i. am 29. IV. 1947

gestorben und am 8. Mai 1947 bestattet wurde:

Papesch Otto

Charakter: ...

Religion: alt. kath. Stand: ...

Wohnort: Wien XIII, ...

Alter: Jahre und Geburtsdatum: 17. II. 1898

Geburtsort: Wien

Heimatsgemeinde: Wien

Todesursache: Tbc

Bestattungsort: Zentralfriedhof

Urkund dessen nachstehende eigenhändige Unterschrift und das beigedrückte Amtssiegel

Wien am 25. November 1947

My father's death certificate, 8 May 1947

I have two vivid recollections of my father. One is of him coming into our children's bedroom to wish us good night. He had his boots on. That must have impressed me. I must have been three years old. My second recollection was when he was still living at home. He again came into our children's bedroom to wish us good night, this time with a bowl of fruit compote that he placed on top of the tall closet by the door as he walked out of the room. I later asked my mother whether I had just been dreaming and she confirmed that he would have put the bowl up high so that we couldn't get to it, tuberculosis being so terribly contagious.

My mother received a letter from a Dr F. B. Trudeau on 29 April 1947 while she was still in the United States. He wrote that he thought she could obtain streptomycin through the firm Merk and Co. or Lilley Company but that he believed it to be quite expensive. She wrote on the bottom in pencil, *You were very kind to answer my letter asking about streptomycin so quickly. My husband died the day your letter reached me. Helas!*

Thank you very much for wanting to help.
Sincerely yours…

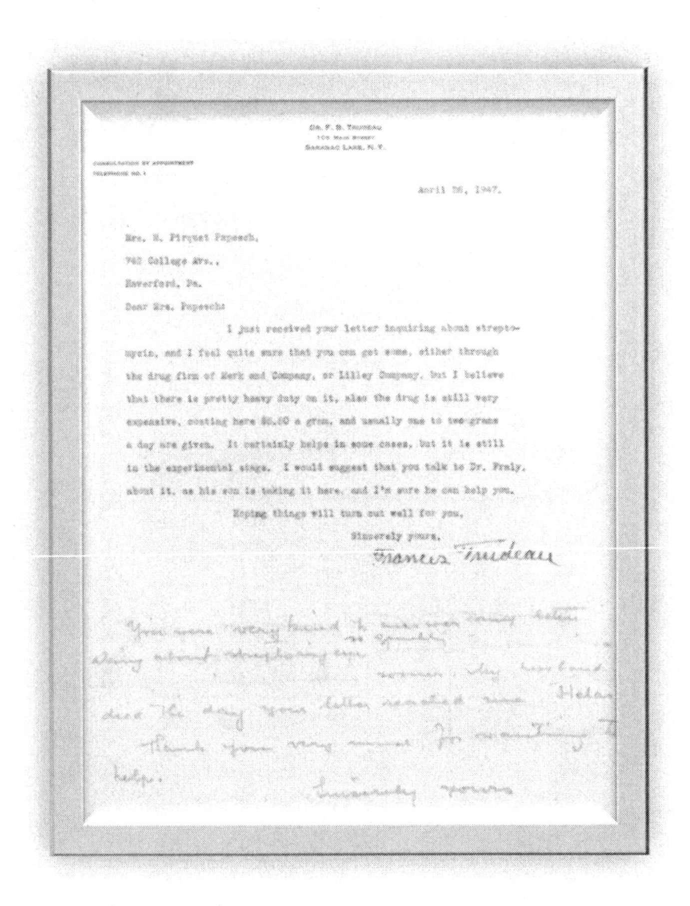

Dr. F. B. Trudeau
Saranac Lake, N.Y.

Consultation by appointment
Telephone No. [illegible]

April 26, 1947.

Mrs. H. Pirquet Papesch,
742 College Ave.,
Haverford, Pa.

Dear Mrs. Papesch:

I just received your letter inquiring about streptomycin, and I feel quite sure that you can get some, either through the drug firm of Merk and Company, or Lilley Company, but I believe that there is pretty heavy duty on it, also the drug is still very expensive, costing here $[illegible] a gram, and usually one to two grams a day are given. It certainly helps in some cases, but it is still in the experimental stage. I would suggest that you talk to Dr. Fraly, about it, as his son is taking it here, and I'm sure he can help you.

Hoping things will turn out well for you,

Sincerely yours,
Frances Trudeau

Letter from Dr F. B. Trudeau dated 26 April and her note upon receiving it on 29 April 1947

On 29 April 1947, my grandmother made a note on the last page of my father's diary dated 12 November 1917: *My poor child, what dread and fear and homesickness your heart must have felt, only to perish as a result of the exertions of war.*

My father's grave in the Zentralfriedhof cemetery in Vienna

Having died so early, my father was never able to get to know his grandchildren but the extraordinary resemblance with the younger of my twins, Thor, allows us to feel his ongoing presence among us.

My father aged 40, 1938

His grandson, Thor Papesch Mulà, aged 40, 2017

His grandson, Lars Papesch Mulà, aged 40, 2017

Appendices

The original German version of this contains excerpts of my father's correspondence (including transcriptions) with his parents and with my mother. His doctoral thesis is held by the Archives of the Technical University of Vienna.

Appendices included here:

1. Grebner Papesch Hrdliczka Family Chronicle (Excerpts)
2. My Father's Wartime Diary: 17 February to 12 November 1917
3. List of Themes
4. List of Drawings
5. My Father's Will
6. Photographic Album of the Invasion of Poland 1939
7. List of Illustrations

1. Grebner Papesch Hrdliczka Family Chronicle (Excerpts)

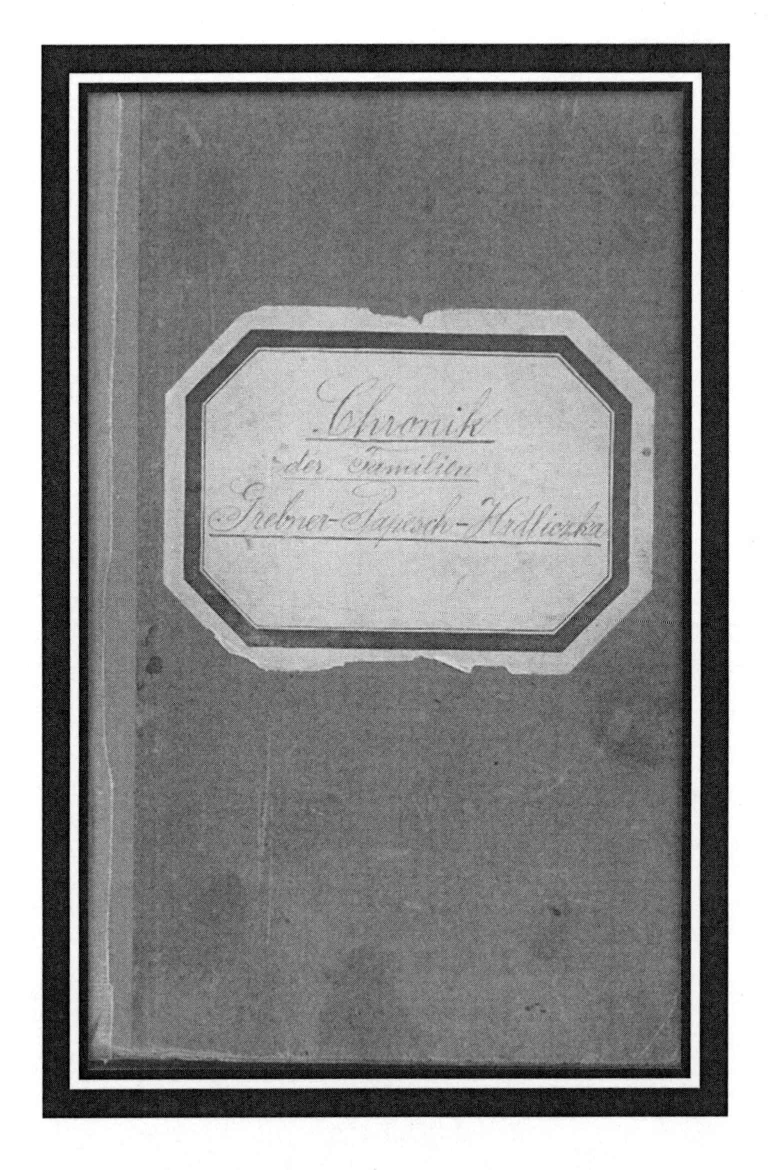

Grebner-Papesch-Hrdliczka Family Chronicle (handwritten booklet by my grandfather, Ottokar Papesch)

Auszug aus dem Familienregister I der kath. Pfarrkirche zu Joh. d. Täufer in Bad Mergentheim, Seite 1676.

laut Trauzeugnis des kath. Pfarramtes in Neckarsulm wurden am 3. Mai 1790 hier getraut:

Bräutigam: Franz Christof Grebner, Justizrat in Kupferzell geboren 14/5 1766

Braut: Franziska Barbara Lindner geboren 16/11 1768

Eltern des Bräutigams: Franz Anton Grebner Amtsobervogt des Deutschen Ritterordens in Ikelheim und seine Frau Therese geb. Kirchgasser

Eltern der Braut: Franz Jos. Lindner, Hofkammerrath des Deutschen Ritter Ordens in Neckarsulm und seine Frau M. Barbara Ulsamer

Sie hatten 14 Kinder

Grebner

I	1.	Franz	geb:	29/3 1791 in Kupferzell † 1851		siehe Seite 4-23
II	2.	Barbara	"	1792	verheiratete Lamel	siehe Seite 26
III	3.	Josefa	"	1793	" Pfaff	" 26
IV	4.	Theresia	"	1794	blieb ledig	" 27
V	5.	Elisabeth	"	1796	verheiratete Becker	" 27
VI	6.	Josef	"	1797		" 27
VII	7.	Karoline	"	1799	verh. Wolf	" 28
VIII	8.	Magdalena	"	1800	† 1800	" 28
IX	9.	Karl Josef	"	1801	† 1804	" 28
X	10.	Thomas	"	1802	† 1868	" 31-44
XI	11.	~~Georg~~	"	1803		" 29
XII	12.	Eleonora	"	1804	blieb ledig (Tante Lore)	" 29
XIII	13.	Johanna	"	1806	verheiratete Ostertag	" 30
XIV	14.	Rosa	"	1808	† 1809	" 30

Grebner-Papesch-Hrdliczka Family Chronicle (handwritten booklet by my grandfather, Ottokar Papesch): Excerpt from the family register 1, 1676

4)

I. Franz von Grebner

* 24/3 1790 in Kupferzell, Württemberg
+ 23/8 1851 in Datschitz in Mähren

hat als Offizier den Zug Napoleons nach Moskau [illegible] und soll einem Baron Dahlberg das Leben gerettet haben. Wurde dann Generalbevollmächtigter des Baron Dahlberg, wurde nach seinem Tod in der Gruft der Dahlberg in Datschitz neben seinem Herrn und Freund begraben. Er baute die erste Zuckerfabrik in [illegible]

seine Frau Helene geborene Goergen
* 29/5 1808 in Wien, getauft Pfarre Alservorstadt
+ 27/6 1905 "

getraut am 28/5 1826 in der Pfarrkirche Gumpendorf
sie lebten später getrennt, da ihr das Leben in Datschitz zu langweilig war. Mit 60 Jahren machte sie noch eine Amerikareise, lebte dann später in [illegible] und kam erst 1 Jahr vor ihrem Tod nach Wien zurück.

* 22/8 1777 / + 29/3 1842 — Der Vater war der Dr. Bruno Goergen, Irrenarzt und Gründer der ersten Irrenanstalt in Döbling
* 4/9 1776 / + 11/10 1848 — die Mutter war Frau Gertraud Schäffer, geb. [illegible], eine Tochter der Frau Katharina Schäffer, [illegible] (diese war [illegible]) aus Aachen,

Franz und Helene Grebner hatten 8 Kinder

	Name		Jahr		Seite
1.	Charlotte (Lotti)	geb.	1827	siehe Seite	5, 6, 7
2.	Karl	"	1828	"	8
3.	Gustav	"	1829	"	8
4	Eduard	"	1830	"	9
5	Emilie	"	1833	"	10
6	Max	"	1836	"	9
7	Franziska	"	1837 + 1838	starb jung	
8	Franziska	"	1838	"	9

Der Vater des Dr. Bruno Goergen war Architekt in Trier in Deutschland

Grebner-Papesch-Hrdliczka Family Chronicle (handwritten booklet by my grandfather, Ottokar Papesch): Franz von Grebner

d) Ferdinand Hrdliczka

Sohn des Peter Hrdliczka siehe Seite 10

* 28/10 1860 in Morawitz in Mähren

\+ 23/11 1942 in Wien

war zuerst Professor an der Photogr. Versuchsanstalt in Wien, dann Gründer und Besitzer einer Fabrik für photographische Platten und Papiere, Gutsbesitzer in Aujezd bei Znaim

verheiratet mit Eleonore Dobrofsky (Lori)

28/8 ? * 12/8 1864

\+ 8/3 1942 in Wien

war die Tochter des Dr. Dobrofski, Arzt in Aujezd bei Znaim und seiner Frau Therese ?

die Ehe blieb kinderlos

Eleonore Dobrofsky war in erster Ehe mit Adolf Robitschek Beamter im Fin. Ministerium verheiratet, aus welcher Ehe eine Tochter Lola Robitschek stammt, die den Artillerie-Oberleutnant Rudolf Spinnler heiratete, welcher als Oberstleutnant in Znaim gestorben ist. Aus dieser Ehe stammen 2 Kinder

Ferdinand Spinnler * \+ 1951 in Wien

verh. mit Elfriede (Elfi) Gerhart, Schauspielerin, die Ehe wurde bald geschieden

und Eleonore (Lorle) Spinnler

verh. mit Ing. Leopold Hengl

auch diese Ehe wurde bald geschieden

Grebner-Papesch-Hrdliczka Family Chronicle (handwritten booklet by my grandfather, Ottokar Papesch): Ferdinand Hrdliczka

e) Paul Hrdliczka
Sohn des Peter Hrdliczka. siehe Seite 10

* 4/5 1863 in Morawetz in Mähren
+ 16/7 1892 in Wien

war Oberleutnant bei einem Infanterie Regiment und Lehrer der Inf. Kadettenschule in Triest

f) Max Hrdliczka siehe Seite 10

* 6/6 1865 in Morawetz in Mähren
+ 30/8 1958 in [illegible]

war zuerst Forstmeister beim Fürsten Salm in Raitz und kam dann nach Strassnitz in Mähren zum Grafen Magnis als Forst- u. Güterdirektor, wo er später Generalbevollmächtigter wurde.
Er gründete eine große Holzimprägnierungs Anstalt in Bistritz am Hostein
verheiratet mit Helene Alder

* 14/2 1871 in Wien
+ 4/7 1929 in Strassnitz in Mähren

sie war die Tochter des Viktor Alder, Besitzer einer chemischen und Kapselfabrik in Wien-Oberlaa und seiner Frau Helene Reisser

Aus dieser Ehe stammen 3 Töchter

Margarete (Grell) verehelichte Preuss (Seite 16)
Elsa " Zöller (" 17)
Marie (Mizzi) " Hones (" 18)

Grebner-Papesch-Hrdliczka Family Chronicle (handwritten booklet by my grandfather, Ottokar Papesch): Max Hrdliczka

19)

g) **Viktor Hrdliczka**

Sohn des Peter Hrdliczka, siehe Seite 10

* 10/9 1867 in Morawetz in Mähren

\+ 22/3 1950 in Wien

Med. Dr., praktischer Arzt in Wien

verheiratet mit **Marie Alder** (Maus)

* 22/4 1880 in Wien

Tochter des Viktor Alder, Besitzer einer Chemischen und Kapselfabrik in Wien-Oberlaa und seiner Frau Marie geborene Kopitsch

Der Ehe entstammen 3 Kinder

Martha, Viktor, Gertrude

Martha Hrdliczka

* 18/3 1901 in Wien

Med. Dr., machte als junge Frau die Matura u. Doktorat

verheiratet mit **Fritz Wahlberg**

* 15/6 1888 in Wien

\+ 13/2 1941 in Wien

war Besitzer einer Maschinenfabrik, starb plötzlich an Herzschlag

Fortsetzung umseitig

Grebner-Papesch-Hrdliczka Family Chronicle (handwritten booklet by my grandfather, Ottokar Papesch): Viktor Hrdliczka (Father), Marie Alder and Martha Hrdliczka

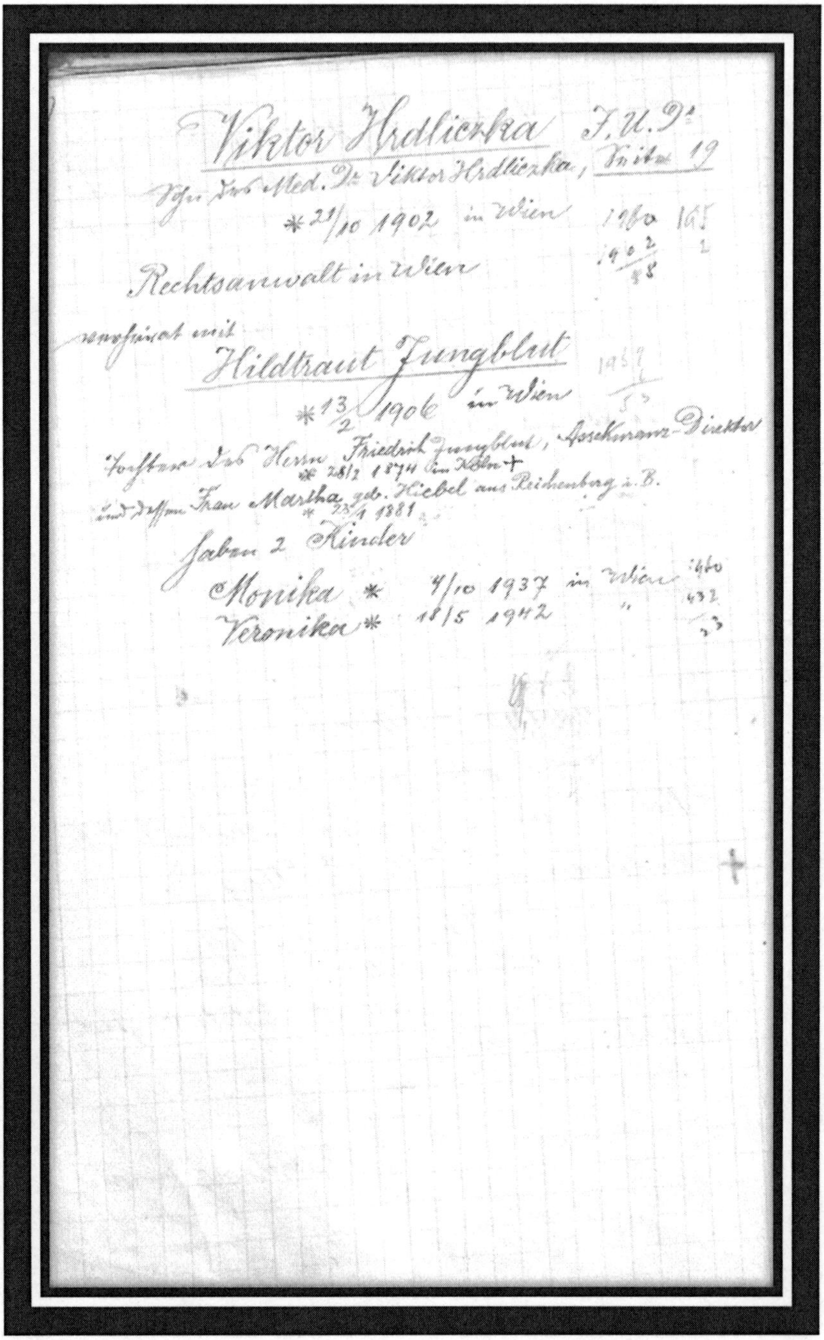

Viktor Hrdliczka J.U.Dr.

Sohn des Med. Dr. Viktor Hrdliczka, Seite 19

* 21/10 1902 in Wien

Rechtsanwalt in Wien

verheiratet mit

Hildtraut Jungblut

* 13/2 1906 in Wien

Tochter des Herrn Friedrich Jungblut, [illegible]-Direktor
* 28/2 1874 in Köln +
und dessen Frau Martha geb. Hiebel aus Reichenberg i. B.
* 23/4 1881

haben 2 Kinder

Monika * 4/10 1937 in Wien

Veronika * 18/5 1942 "

Grebner-Papesch-Hrdliczka Family Chronicle (handwritten booklet by my grandfather, Ottokar Papesch): Viktor Hrdliczka (Son)

21

Gertrud Hrdliczka

Tochter des Med. Dr. Viktor Hrdliczka   Seite 19

* 30/7 1904 in Wien

Musikdirigentin, verheiratet mit

Ing. Werner Hofmann * 8/2 1900 in New York

Spezialist im Bau von Ölraffinerien

Lernten sich in Baku kennen, wo Werner eine russische Ölraffinerie für eine amerikanische Firma baute und Trude auf einer Konzerttournee durch Sowjetrussland [illegible] in Baku dirigierte

haben 1 Sohn

Peter Kurt Hofmann * 2/10 1932 in Wien
\+ 20/7 1952 in New York
an akuter Leukämie. Er studierte Forstwirtschaft

Hofmanns übersiedelten [illegible] Jahre 1967 von New York nach [illegible]

Grebner-Papesch-Hrdliczka Family Chronicle (handwritten booklet by my grandfather, Ottokar Papesch): Gertrud Hrdliczka

34

Emilie Grebner

* 5/10 1841 in Suchdol in Böhmen
\+ 6/9 1926 in Prag

Tochter des Thomas Grebner, siehe Seite 31
heiratete i. J. 1865, 25/9 in ~~Laschan~~ Mühlhausen bei Kralup a. Moldau

Eduard Papesch

* 18/1 1835 in Welwarn
\+ 4/1 1888 in Prag

Sohn des Wenzel Papesch, Kaufmann in Welwarn
war Direktor der Montan- u. Industriewerke in Bras, Pilsen, Zbirov etc. in der Zentrale in Prag

Der Ehe entstammten 7 Kinder

1. Emilie Franziska Papesch siehe hierfür
2. Eduard " siehe Seite 35
3. Ottokar } Zwillinge " " 36
4. Wladimir " " 35
5. Franziska " " 41
6. Emilie " " 41
7. Rosa " " 42

1. Emilie Franziska Papesch

Tochter des Eduard Papesch
* 4/3 1866 in Prag
\+ 24/7 1866 " "

Grebner-Papesch-Hrdliczka Family Chronicle (handwritten booklet by my grandfather, Ottokar Papesch): Emilie Grebner and Eduard Papesch

Emilie Grebner (1841-1926), my father's paternal grandmother

Eduard Papesch (1835-88), my father's paternal grandfather

36

Ottokar Papesch

Sohn des Eduard Papesch siehe Seite 34

* 23/11 1868 in Prag

als Zwillingsbruder des Wladimir Papesch

† 29.2.1960 in Wien

war Oberinspektor der Österr. Nationalbank in Wien

verheiratet mit

Marie Hrdliczka

* 14/11 1872 in Morawetz in Mähren

† 24.10.1963 in Wien

war die Tochter des Peter Hrdliczka

siehe Seite 10 und Seite 22

Die Trauung war am 19/2 1898 in der Pfarrkirche St. Othmar im III. Bezirk

aus der Ehe entstammen 2 Söhne

Otto Papesch siehe Seite 37

Viktor Papesch " " 39

Otto Papesch machte nach der Kriegsmatura im Jahre 1916 die Ausbildung bei den 30.5 Mörsern in Budapest mit, ging dann nach Rumänien und später an die italienische Front am Monte Grappa und kam Oktober 1918 nach Wien. Machte an der Technik den Ingenieur, später schon im Dienst bei der Firma Rainer Hrdliczka das Doktorat der Photochemie. Im Jahre 1941 machte er als Offizier den Feldzug gegen Polen mit, erkrankte darauf und wurde in Grimmenstein nach 1½ jähr. Erholung des Militärs eingestellt. Erkrankte im Jahre 1946 neuerdings an Lungentuberkulose und starb tief betrauert am 29/4 47.

Grebner-Papesch-Hrdliczka Family Chronicle (handwritten booklet by my grandfather, Ottokar Papesch): Ottokar Papesch and Marie Hrdliczka

Otto Papesch

Sohn des Ottokar Papesch siehe Seite 17

* 17/11 1898 in Wien
\+ 29/4 1947 " " im Lainzer Kkhaus.

ist Dr. Ing. Chemiker

machte nach der Kriegsmatura den ersten Weltkrieg in Rumänien und Italien mit, war dann 17 Jahre bei seinem Onkel Ferdinand Hrdliczka in der Fabrik für Photopapiere u. Platten, später kurze Zeit bei der Photofirma Kilophot.
Im Jahre 1941 rückte er wieder ein und machte den Feldzug gegen Polen mit, wo er erkrankte, war 1½ Jahre in Grimmenstein Tbc Heilanstalt
Im Jahr kam er zur Wiener Film A.G.
welche im Krieg zerstört wurde. (später wieder saniert)

verheiratet mit 6. Juni 1931
Margarete Pirquet

* 14/10 1903 in Wien

Der Ehe entstammen 2 Kinder
Peter Papesch * 19/7 1938
Christine Papesch * 29/4 1943

Grebner-Papesch-Hrdliczka Family Chronicle (handwritten booklet by my grandfather, Ottokar Papesch): Otto Papesch and Margarete Pirquet

20

Viktor Papesch

Sohn des Ottokar Papesch siehe Seite 17

* 26/1 1905 in Wien IV 5

er ist Ing. Chemiker, nach seinen Studien war er beim Onkel Viktor Alder in Oberlaa und ging dann nach Chicago in U. S. A. wo er in der Heilmittelfabrik Searle seit dem Jahre 1930 beschäftigt ist.

Verheiratet mit Mary Marczyk

* 17/11 1908 in Denver in U. S. A.

Sie studierte Musik in Wien, nahm Klavierstunden beim Rosenthal, lehrte in der Musikakademie in Philadelphia

Sie heirateten am 14/8 1930 in Wien III in der Pfarrkirche St. Othmar

haben 1 Kind

Roger Papesch

* 29/5 1936 in Chicago U. S. A.

Grebner-Papesch-Hrdliczka Family Chronicle (handwritten booklet by my grandfather, Ottokar Papesch): Viktor Papesch and Mary Marczyk

2. My Father's Wartime Diary: 17 February to 12 November 1917

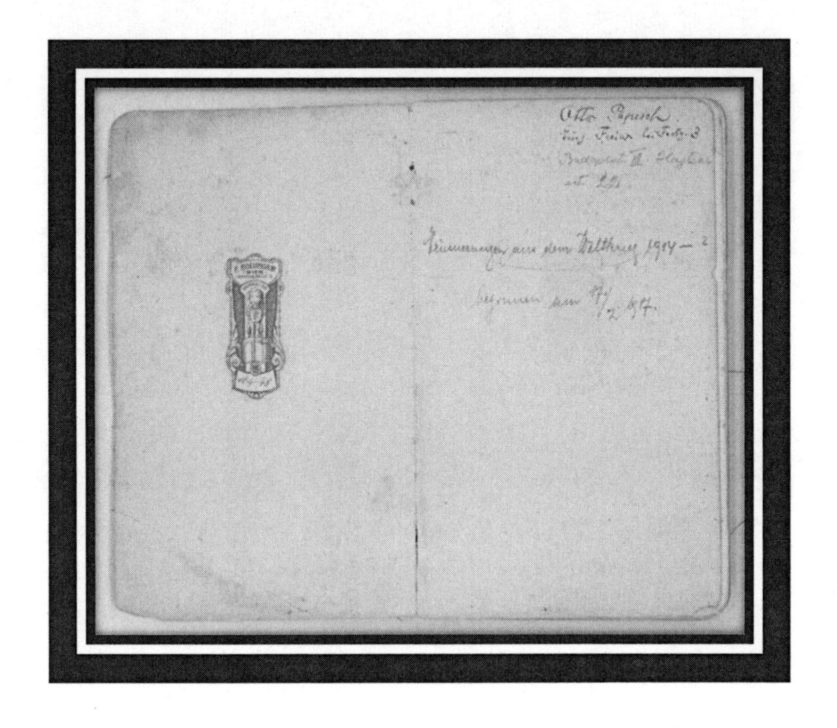

My father's notebook: "Otto Papesch First Year at Feotz 3 Budapest VII. Hajtsar Nt 22"

Recollections of the World War 1914
Begun on 17.2.1917

In order to start I need to go back a little to the last few days. After my and Lazansky's… [*half of the page was erased]*. The hour of the goodbyes from my parents was to be on a bleak February morning. Both behaved very courageously and I think I did too despite the fact that I had a lump in my throat. A controller must have thrown away our 2nd Class tickets because we had to travel to Graz in 3rd Class railroad cars. Apart from lunch in Hotel W… and a few other banalities, I enjoyed our stay in Graz. My feisty companion, Jonczi Musger, showed me a few tourist attractions of the town. We luckily had fine weather and visited the lookout at Hilm Lake and then hiked through some lovely woods to Maria Trost. There was little to be seen on the Pensionisten Glacier Schloßerg apart from the big clock tower. Everything was enveloped in fog. After a horrendous trip we arrived in Laibach [Lubjana] and were housed in quarters outside of town. We were allowed to eat in the officer's mess for lunch and dinner. I mention this because it contradicted my pessimistic expectations. There was little bread to be had, or none. Our stomachs growled either because of the change of air or because of roaming around doing nothing. After 3 days we received the orders to leave for... Vienna. We weren't exactly ecstatic about these orders. Rumours and tales about being sent to France swirled around in our heads. We managed to obtain 3 loaves of bread for each one of us – it is difficult to describe how happy I was with those loaves! If someone had told me a year ago that I would be ecstatic with 3 loaves of bread under my arm I'd have laughed in his face. Yes, the military makes you humble. We are now sitting in a mixed freight train.

We expect to reach Vienna in 27 hours. There can be no greater joy than riding in a 2nd Class carriage with fellow soldiers and listen to a strange concert of snoring, wheezing, grating teeth. A staff sergeant's description of episodes on the Italian front didn't exactly lift our spirits. However, I won't believe anything till I've seen it with my own eyes. The future will tell. [*Next sentence illegible*]. As I have absolutely no illusions about going to the front I hope therefore to be able to overcome many things.

18 February 1917, 3 a.m., Graz Railway Station

We arrived in Graz after 19 hours. Such a mixed freight train is a real pain. I long for this trip to be over soon. I would gladly let someone else spend the night with two other people, one of whom is quite nice, the other absolutely objectionable. My dear diary, I shall take my feelings about fiscal matters to my grave. I owe the state some thanks for this type of trip for it gets rid of my beef about train travel. It wouldn't be everyone's cup of tea to travel by rail between 1200 and 1400 km in 10 days. It was quite a feat. Dear God please provide us with an express train! The southbound railways are an unsurmountable barrier even if the roads and paths were to be empty.

18 March 1917, Vienna, Schwarzenberg Barracks

Dear Diary, forgive me for having neglected you for so long, but when one can spend a whole month in Vienna and have almost nothing to do, one thinks of other things than scribbling down one's "experiences".

After spending a few days in coffee houses, we were handed over to the 31st mortar battery in order to undergo training, which meant that I was free in the afternoon. After 3 weeks of this idyllic state of affairs we were returned to our old battery. I would have liked to stay with No. 31, be it only for the relationship that officers have with the cadets. The first honour bestowed upon me was that I was named the day's corporal once. Thank goodness I received some guidance from a kind soul who knew his way around. Instead of writing about my duties I will make a parenthesis here. Thanks to some cigarettes and some nice words I went to the theatre.

I rushed back to the barracks and told the inspector, offering him a few cigarettes, that I was suffering terribly from sleepless nights. And so I spent the night in the fireworks room and slept quite well despite the noise and awful smell. This wonderful time is drawing to a close. We are supposed to leave in a fortnight. We will be getting new artillery and vehicles and won't be waiting for the old ones to be repaired. Too bad that I won't be seeing Papa any more. *"Muß i den, muß I den zum Städtle hinaus"* [German folk song]. Farewell again for a while, dear diary.

18 April 1917

As I described in my previous notes, there didn't seem to be any prospect of being sent to the front. However, it has been confirmed that we will be sent out on 1 May. Ammunition, guns and vehicles are ready to move out within days. I am in a miserable state of mind – I am neither happy nor unhappy about this news. I would actually prefer the latter rather than this endless feeling of uncertainty. One suffers it in order to survive. I'm not thrilled, but interested. I'm not thrilled because I would like to see the end of this yet unforeseeable war. Most of those poor devils paid dearly for their enthusiasm. Our chief is turning out to be an ideal commander, very strict when on duty but with a warm heart that expands when he's had a bit of speck. Enough for today and also for when I'm in Vienna. I will give you something to chew on when I'm back out in the field.

20 May 1917

After taking hasty leave we set off after 24 hours and arrived in Maros Vasarhely *[the market town of Marosvasarhely in what is today central Romania, Transylvania in my father's time]* after 3 days. We were ordered to leave the train here and find our own transport to Nyarad Szent Laszlo. I had a delightful experience during the trip. I was on one of the lighter vehicles and so arrived in a village quite some time ahead of schedule. Some comrades of mine and I set out to find something to eat. A number of village people, all dressed up, were standing around one of the larger houses of the town. As we passed them they invited us to partake in the wedding celebrations. We accepted after having performed some conventional affectations and returned to our car about half an hour later with stomachs filled to the brim. The physically handicapped groom accompanied us. It was clear that the bride was in expecting circumstances. Country-style hospitality. Berger, Musger and I are now staying in a small house that leans to one side having been windswept for years. You'd think we were in paradise. Geese, ducks and chickens run around on the streets, people sell eggs, butter, milk etc. for little money. We city folk that have gone without such delights for so long stuff ourselves as much as we can. The children are all quite beautiful. Most important will be that this lazing around will count as military duty at the front.

23 May 1917

H…, I… and I had to lay the telephone line to the observation tower. We had to go back and forth twice. There were about 80 field commander "dudes" (as our old man calls them) here today to witness Big Bertha blasting off. 2 German generals with the distinction of *Pour le mérite* were also in attendance. The launch wasn't as forceful as I had thought but the howling that ensued was absolutely indescribable and weird the like of which I've never heard before. One thing touches me in a strange way: wild orgies with some foul prostitute are underway up on top while our little trio is carrying out discussions about some rather serious matters.

26 May 1917

These lovely exercises have now finished. It certainly was a day that will forever figure in our memories. We had fine weather and General Rohr came to our lookout stand with the two Germans, Seekt and Litzmann, as well as with a number of officers. The entire "Corona" proceeded to the shelter for lunch, some 400 metres from the enemy line – us included. The barrage against this position started on the dot of 2.30 p.m. The assault troops began to push into enemy trenches after 15 minutes of this destructive shooting spree. This barrage fire that I heard for the first time in my life made a big impression on me. The howling and cracking noise of the projectiles took my breath away since this was the first time I ever witnessed such a thing. I had also ventured out a bit too far and some bits of the explosives fell near me. That was my baptism by fire - not enemy fire but by our own fire. There were no casualties except for a captain having been wounded the previous day. Such accidents often lead to casualties and fatalities during this type of exercise, so this was really quite an exception.

27 May 1917

We're being ordered to decamp from this idyllic little nest. The people are so friendly here that it will be hard to say farewell. The local folk detested the Germans for their autocratic behaviour. A few nice words and you could get them to do any service or favour for you.

29 May 1917

Our departure from Nyarad St Laszlo turned out to be a huge flower show. People carrying bouquets came out from every house. We and even our vehicles were hung with entire gardens. Unfortunately, these decorations dried up quickly in the hot summer sun and fell off. We stayed in Maros Vasarhely for half a day and then got put into trains again and left. I travelled on the open car so as to be able to see this wonderful countryside. There is something quite charming about this Transylvania. The lower hills seemed to frame the Alps towards evening and the region became more and more mountainous. More and more mountain tops covered with snow appeared meaning that they must be quite high. In the end it got cold and I went down to get my coat and reserve a secure place to sleep. We then landed in a railway station where there was a long train filled to the brim with Bosniaks. Then suddenly there appeared a face in the darkness that I didn't recognise at first, Kurt Hofmann. The poor devil is being sent to the Isonzo. I hope he doesn't finish up like poor Eckhardt. What a coincidence!

1 June 1917

We arrived in Berezk on 30 May and were offloaded from 3 a.m. to 10 a.m. We 6 cadets were given a large clean room and we immediately set out to ennoble the human exterior by washing when our idyllic tranquillity was suddenly interrupted at 7.30 p.m. with the order that we were to leave for the position on the Gitos Pass at 9 p.m. I had a variety of special mishaps as for example being unable to find someone to carry my stuff to the car but I did manage to make the departure on time. It was a starry night and the moon was half full so that one could see the road quite clearly despite the fact that we had to travel with dimmed lights to avoid the enemy spotting us. Four of the blown-up bridges were lit up and appeared like huge ghosts in the warm night air. After having travelled for about 2 hours the many flares that lit the night were an indication that we couldn't be far from the front. The team immediately set to work and I got up onto a hilltop to see if I could make out the enemy. Then suddenly the alert of an enemy plane was given. The defence artillery stationed in the surrounding mountains immediately sent up greetings of their own. However, the plane was flying too high and just carried on travelling on its way. I was part full of joy, part very angry at it appearing. On the one hand it was the first enemy I had ever seen, on the other I found it an insult that it should fly over our beautiful Transylvania. If I hadn't been ashamed to mention this to my companions and if I'd been alone I'd have taken a rock and thrown it up at that plane, no matter that it was flying about 3km above me. This might sound childish but can be explained. My baptism by fire occurred when those enemy scoundrels fired some shrapnel into our shelter. There wasn't any damage. I have been allocated to the cannon. So be it.

8 June 1917

After building the Lizzi shelter for the last two days we had to return to Berezk. Enemy lines are only 50 metres from ours. Our captain refused to take the responsibility for the possible scattering of short shots from the cannon as each one can fire 2000 a round. We had to set up the cannons in the vicinity of Berezk. 11 shots were fired into a target. 11 shots at 2000 R are 22000 R… there is a need for absolute control. Who pays for that? The state does but I do indirectly and in the future my children probably will. The exercise was a success. There wasn't too much scattering. We then continued the construction work. I'm homesick for the first time in my life. I've been away from my parents several times already but never among only strangers. My opinion about my value in this war is becoming clearer and clearer. I'm a nothing. I can only depend on myself alone because not even a friend would help me in situations like these here. I'm fighting for my existence and quite definitely want to come out the victor in this battle. My stomach still hasn't recovered from the chow. It is shameful that the bread that you get in Romania is made from corn and potatoes, is often mouldy and has been nibbled on by mice. I now know why I get along so well with Murgen because he often has the same point of view as me. I received the order today to report to the battery command as observer. After a terrible climb I now sit at a height of 1020 metres and have a spectacular view of Romania. You can see one observer after the other, all badly disguised. I think there is a tacit understanding not to shoot at the observers from either sides. I'm slowly getting over my homesickness and am feeling a strong incentive to get home in good health which is helping me get through such sad moments. We will get another set of injections tomorrow and the day after. I'll hide if they try to force me. They say the best immunisation is to drink water. That is particularly important around here because there are still plenty of corpses and horse cadavers lying around in the woods.

9 June 1917

The beautiful weather is leaving me. It started raining yesterday evening and rained throughout the night. We'd have drowned in our make-shift hut if I and my other two telephone specialists hadn't covered the posts of our tents with a tarpaulin so that most of the water that had seeped in could run off again on one side. We also covered the shelter with hay on which we slept till late next morning. Although our hut didn't have a door and although there was a draft like in a bird cage and although mice were running around on the ground and up to our beds and although it was bitterly cold due to the altitude we were at, we nevertheless slept like alley cats. I only got up at 11 a.m. – what else was there to do? Food was ice cold but our hungry stomachs couldn't care less. It was with great appetite that I downed the black gunk called coffee and what used to be called *Zwieback* (rusk). The sun finally came out at 1 p.m. so that we once again had a magnificent 360 degree view over the land. You have to be really careful where you tread because there are still many unexploded bombs etc. lying around. The festivities must be starting in Straßnitz now – why couldn't I be there too?

11 June 1917

I returned to Lizzi after having been relieved from my post. I spent a lot of time thinking of Straßnitz. I heard all sorts of titbits about underhanded manoeuvring in the distribution of food and this from people you'd think wouldn't be able to put two and two together. I don't want to believe all of them till I don't get proof but where there's smoke there's also fire. If it were true that our hard working team was robbed of its rightful portions of food (what else could you call them?) then you'd call it pure and simple street robbery and nothing else! We're doing nothing but laze around. As long as this is classified as official duty at the front.

14 June 1917

On the 12th of this month I was ordered to go to Berezk to organise hooded habits. They came out great and were much appreciated. It just annoys me that my work is taken for granted in this way. I travelled there by car and also by cable-car. The last trip was particularly wonderful. What a joy and great feeling if you don't suffer from vertigo to hover over the landscape this way. In Berezk I was once again able to get something to eat – I need to point this out as it is becoming a rare event! Back at the shelter it's back to the same old same old: awful bread that looks like cow dung, is heavy like lead, smells mostly like castor oil and tastes foul. And let's not speak of quantities. We received 1 ¼ loaves of bread for 3 days. It's too little for me who is not doing hard labour. How the others cope is a mystery to me. If only I were a *Fähnrich* already! Nothing much new otherwise. Our work has stalled because our vehicles aren't allowed to drive over the pass because the road hasn't been looked after and wouldn't be able to cope with the steel tyres. Cold rainy weather. In the field you learn to appreciate living in a nice house with enough food to eat. If only there were peace again or at least to be expected in a short while, then you could suffer all these pains.

16 June 1917

I don't want to start writing about food again but it was a great joy to receive a package from the wedding in Straßnitz. I'm almost ashamed to say this but the sapper lieutenant with whom I'm living offered me his supper ration after he saw me down a second cup of coffee for my evening meal. He had already eaten elsewhere. I accepted it although I would have never dreamed of doing that under other circumstances. Needs must when the devil drives. The letter I received from Mamma today is really worrying me because she writes she wants to send Papa to the doctor for examinations. I hope nothing is wrong with my old little dad. I'm not usually this emotional but it really hit me today. I hope, God willing, he has many happy years ahead of him. Tomorrow I'm back on the observation post. I hope there will be nice weather again. Those scoundrel Russians shoot at any man that appears on the terrain. That is how a 52-year-old sapper, who wanted to be discharged shortly, got badly wounded. How unlucky!

20 June 1917

I'm back at my observation post and the weather god is good to me. It's beautiful up here, an idyllic summer holiday. When observing nature I often forget that it's war. My other comrades think of nothing else except what there's to eat. They're justified not to speak of anything else. The food is awful and there's little of it. We don't see anything of what are supposed to be our rations. They get lost somewhere. How could people not be angry? My heart sinks when I see people anxiously awaiting every crumb of foul corn bread in order to make it to the next day. How do you match up the minister for the food supply of the population giving people his fatherly advice not to send food parcels to the front as the soldiers are apparently looked after very well while the soldiers out here are begging for bread or asking to find and buying some at all cost? Yes, when you're sitting around a nicely set table it's easy to give advice to those who are forced to "hang in there" etc. I'd just like to know where the money for our provisions disappears to. Today is the 5th week of this cadet's longing for something to eat. It's a godsend that I can buy a loaf of bread for a large sum of money now and then. With that I can take the edge off my hunger. Our chief commander, the German General Gerock, is supposed to come for an inspection today.

30 June 1917

We cadets are now going through our cycle with each one having to do sketches of our surroundings from either the observation or the reconnaissance posts. It's a new definition for lazing around. We can't complain about having to work too much. We could accept these conditions if they were to stay like this. In two months this cadet detention of ours will be over. No more lazing around after that. Things look awful here on the recce post. There must have been a horrific battle here. My thoughts about whether to choose photo chemistry or forestry preoccupy me for the moment. Now that food rations have improved you tend to forget there's a war on in these beautiful natural surroundings.

2 July 1917

This year I will be celebrating my names day on the reconnaissance post. It's a day like any other but you still think about how things used to be and how they are now. I had an exciting hunt for mice during the night. These seemingly sweet little animals run around all night and up the wall to the rucksacks and bread pouches and eat up our small rations. They are an undesirable presence here. I often stumble across corpses covered with a bit of grass or branches and with blowflies buzzing around when I'm on one of my recce expeditions up here. A dog is treated better. It's amazing that this rabble can't do it. I've been given permission to go to the parking lot for one night - that means for two days. Two days of living a decent life.

16 July 1917

After spending 2 days on the parking lot doing my duties I got back to the battery and straight to the battery command. I was informed that our former group commander, a captain, was sacked because of having embezzled government funds. One day later we cadets got the order to assemble at the command in order to be assigned to observation, reconnaissance, etc. positions. I and one of my comrades have been assigned to either the telephone or gas officers group. We get treated here like dogs, not like future officers. We get yelled at for the slightest thing. Two officer adjutants get to sleep in a lovely room while three of our kind sleep in a hole where the floor is flooded and where we get hounded to inspect the wiring when it's raining cats and dogs, etc. What an undignified life! I can't write any of this to my parents or they would get even more upset. We suddenly got the order from the top command that our battery will also be deployed because they anticipate an attack and I got shooed off to Jonezi's reconnaissance post. I got a bit scared at first to be sent out to the front trench. The reconnaissance post was more of an observation positioning as it was no further up front than ours. So things were getting serious. I got my things and told the captain I was going. Neither he nor any of the other officers even uttered a sound, so I left. As I had a heavy back pack it took me ¾ of a day to get to my position. I passed through a delightful Romanian Kurvet Slanic that has a bit of an oriental air about it. The dainty village looked abandoned. Some parts had been damaged or covered in soot. The baths that hadn't been totally destroyed were now occupied by soldiers. The mighty casino was totally empty as was the concert pavilion that stands in front of it. Telephone cables criss-crossed through the park. It's a sad sight in these parts of the world. After an exhausting climb up about 1000 metres I arrived at the Baron's, but not before having had to ask for directions how to get there. From there 2 men helped me carry my things and so I finally got to my position. After resting a short while I had to return to the Baron to ask for a gas mask. Hurrah! I was informed that I would be getting officer rations! It is impossible to make a comparison between how our lot get treated and how infantry officers treat us. The major I had to go and greet welcomed me and extended a friendly hand and gave me a few good recommendations. Our captain has never done such a thing. And so I'm here with Tonezi and don't give a damn about the battery with which I have to communicate 3 times a day to inform them of the current situation. The Russians haven't bothered us till now. There are only 5 enemy batteries across from us that shoot at our forward outpost. If ever they should break through our position it will be difficult to escape. What a delight to get these officer's rations compared with the animal feed we've had till now. Soup, meat, an entrée and dessert on top of that. You only realise what a stomach really is till you've had little and bad food and you then get this. I prefer being here with this group despite it being a more dangerous position than with the other group and the lousy food.

20 July 1917

Time is rushing by. I feel physically much stronger due to good food and plenty of it. The attack by the Russians that has now been announced x number of times has not eventuated. Sometimes there is so much work that you feel you're drowning. The observation post that was started by another battery and which we were supposed to replace is absolutely useless for what we need. We had to look for a narrow ditch. We don't even have our own team to carry out the work so have had to rely on friendly sappers to help us. In the meantime, we carried out our observations at the post of a German mountain cannon battery. The very friendly German commander allows us to use his telescope several times during the day. We will need to rely on him for quite a while longer as our observation post won't be ready for another 3-4 weeks. We are six men in our accommodation, so it's a bit crammed, but at least it is water tight. You lose a lot of your repulsion out here…your every sense of niceness. My wash basin is a pool from which I first have to fish out the tortoises before washing. Joneczi washes in his billy and then eats from it. Shoes haven't been touched by a rag not to speak of a brush for 2-3 weeks. That doesn't matter as they get a certain colour little by little so that nothing much changes after you've trampled through mud. Most of us are growing long beards, I a goatee. Who cares, no one looks at us here. Others look exactly the same and even if you wanted to clean up a bit, you'd be dirty again in no time.

22 July 1917

We got the order the day before yesterday to present ourselves in Soosmuzö yesterday at 8 a.m. in order to try on gasmasks. We had already collected our gasmasks from the Baron but we had to go to Soosmuzö anyway despite having protested. Having done our duty we once again turned our backs to the Gjtoz Valley and marched home. We had a quick bath in Slanic and then started off on our climb to the Cheschnidni base. My hunger pangs quickly set in despite having had breakfast and lunch so that when I got back to our post I devoured my breakfast, lunch and dinner rations in one go. I was hoping to be able to sleep in. Instead the 'Russkies' started shooting at us at 5.30 a.m. extending the attack over our surrounding peaks. I needed to get to the German observation post which was about 200 metres away in order to obtain details when that wretch started shooting in my direction. A bit of fear leapt up inside me but there was nothing to be done so I crept out like a monkey and got on my way. The way down was easy but not the way back up. No sooner had I left the German than a few more *"Kleffer"* came my way. *"Kleffer"* is what we call those little enemy projectiles. I ducked behind a mound when things exploded around me, parts of trees, splinters, screeching loudly through the air and then falling with a thud. All went well. Nothing happened to me. I waited a few moments and then continued behind the mound that shielded me. Another few jumps and I arrived in the hut and let out a deep sigh. This isn't exactly the easy life. I calmed down once we were given our lunch ration. Our small hilltop alone received 300 medium calibre shots so far.

25 July 1917

These unmelodious sounds continued like this throughout the afternoon till we had received a total of about 700 shots. The Russians began again as early as 4 a.m. the next morning - a brutal way to wake us up. They continued shooting and unloading about 700 shots onto our little hilltop alone. The surrounding peaks got just as many rounds of fire. When asked about casualties there were only one fatality, one post destroyed and a few wounded. People around here are quite smart and just sit in their dugouts as long as there is shooting. We don't need to do that because our hut is behind a steep slope. If the scoundrel doesn't use a howitzer we have nothing to fear. As soon as there are a few minutes reprieve either Joneszi or I hurry over to the German observation post in order to get information. If there's more shooting we stay there till the next intermission. After that we sprint back into our hut. Yesterday things were decisively calmer with a daily total of just 150-200 Russian rounds of fire. Lunch does get interrupted when shrapnel is buzzing around your ears, but one does get used to that too. A cheeky Russian patrol came snooping up to our dugouts but departed again after our infantry fired some shots at them. A mortar that was transported up here fired 3 harmless control shots. That infuriated the Russians to such an extent that they bathed us from 6 to 7 a.m. with about 150 shots from their artillery. The Russians are getting more active in neighbouring areas too. Either they attack our positions or we fire shots into their trenches. I wonder when they'll start attacking our hilltop.

27 July 1917

I made the disagreeable discovery that our hilltop is more than an outpost and that it is actually a little stronghold. There are only weak posts surrounding this mountain top and communications between the other posts is carried out by mere field guards. I have to confess that I'm a bit worried again, the more so as I observed heavy troop movements in the Saraii Valley yesterday. The artillery trench is only 5 feet away from our dugout…! If there's an attack you can shoot back without getting out of bed and head straight to heaven. It was stupid of Musger and me to have declined the battery commander's offer to relieve us. Let's hope that what we fear doesn't eventuate or we'd be on our way to Siberia the following day or ….?! The battery has suffered a few fatalities. It has had a weird effect on me. People with whom you spoke only yesterday and together were hoping for peace soon are now cold and stiff lying under the earth. I was hit by some small shrapnel yesterday. It only grazed my jacket. But it certainly was a *memento mori.* Later I felt like a bony hand resting where I got hit calling out and saying "Be more careful!" The artillery shots have eased off a bit today.

29 July 1917

Today we had a Sunday in every sense of the word. The morning air was clear and brisk. Not even a rifle shot could be heard. For lunch a real gourmet dinner with 2 meat dishes. The day was over in no time. We didn't have such a calm day yesterday. The news of our victory in Galicia was countered with the bad news the Russians aren't far from us in the Putua and Susi Valleys. We all lost our heads and started to pack up. The others with more experience than us were packing up also so we thought why shouldn't we do the same. A storm in a tea cup. Our mortars remained where they were on the pass. As long as they're not moving back we won't either. I now have had 2 ½ months of field duty.

2 August 1917

There's a full moon tonight and I'm sitting in the door of our hut waiting for recce news. Things were calm up to yesterday, but in the afternoon there was lively shooting towards our summit. No big deal if grenades explode 10 or 100 metres away from you. I'll stay in the dugout as long as it's not my turn to be the observer. Shrapnel can't reach me here. A number of infantrymen (who were lying low in their dugouts like everyone else during the heavy shooting these last few days) received the bronze bravery medal for "courageous behaviour during drumfire". We mortals (who had to be on our post to observe the gunner of one of the mortars, get bombarded with 12cm grenades, weren't allowed to run away and had then to look for the rupture in the telephone wiring under heavy 7.5cm battery fire, etc.) didn't receive the slightest thing. In the end what's important is to be able to see peace alive. That's all I wish for. Our battery officers are now very friendly on the phone to Musgor and me. It must have impressed them that we declined to be relieved from our post here. If only they knew that I did it in order not to be too close to them. Having said that, there are some nice officers who treat us as members of a team. The day will come when I will be a *Fähnrich (*officer candidate). Away from this battery! I'm so happy to have made my choice to study photo chemistry! If only war could be over by October so I could start my courses. I love my one-person photo lab here as opposed to that in the "bunkers" of relatives or acquaintances. I just overheard a telephone conversation. Major preparations are underway for an offensive. An advance would be right since we're having such great weather. Oh well... we shall soon see!

10 August 1917

The big offensive has begun and our side is in full swing. The barrage against enemy lines already began at 5 a.m. on the 8th of the month and continued, sometimes with greater, sometimes with lesser impetus until evening. It was then moved along further with the start of infantry barrage. We only heard later if this was a success. There were also beginnings of movement in my sector. The Russian post in the Sarasii Valley a bit on the left from us was taken by us shortly after some preparatory shots. Only increased artillery fire and mines were directed towards -o-956. This was intended to mislead the enemy as the conditions for an attack were unfavourable. Fierce fighting (the Russians and Romanians defended themselves valiantly) continued on into the night. We had a wonderful view of the battles from our hill top. The positions were bathed in a sea of magnesium light. At the start of the nocturnal battles we were able to notice numerous of our flares go up into the air. Request by the infantry for support from the artillery. The artillery barrage then started blaring during the night (noise twice as awesome in the dark) countering the enemy attack. Now and then there was infantry and also artillery fire when the Russians tried their luck again to attack our positions under cover of darkness. Soon it went quiet again except for a few nervous shots from our posts. The artillery battle began again next morning at the same time as the day before. What I didn't like was that a stray shot from our own artillery would sometimes hit our post. On one occasion it wouldn't have taken much for one of those grenades to land in our shelter. It would have meant going up to heaven right then and there. The Russians began midmorning to fire infantry shots on –o-956 that soon moved on to our hill top. I had just gone to a raised hideout on a tall pine tree when bullets started whistling around our ears. We climbed down the tree in record time! We crouched down behind some large trunks and waited till the shooting was over. The same thing happened to us that night. We were outside again in order to view the nocturnal battles when the Russians attacked our base station. We again leaped behind some thick birch trees. It became damn uncomfortable when the Russians decided to direct some artillery shots toward us. We wanted to escape back to the shelter so as not to get hit, but then another bullet blasted into the tree trunk. So there was another plan change. But after a while we did decide to run for it and get back to our hut where we could be relatively safe. It got quiet soon after, but we stayed put in order to gain our strengths as we would soon need to go back to our battery. Our shelter is so isolated that you can't hear anything of what is going on outside. The only thing you do hear is news about some other victory which we quickly lap up, irrespective if it's true or not. Anyway, during such an offensive you get into a state of what I'd almost call madness. It is something quite mysterious that only a person would understand that has experienced this inner jubilation himself, a state that a realist such as me would even describe with the phrase "to die for the fatherland".

How many times the Almighty has already protected us can be seen by the following incident. Our predecessor from M.Bt.30 had sappers start the construction of one of the observation posts and we let them continue on with it. Suddenly there was news that we'd be going back. The sappers then suddenly disappeared and we had to continue the construction work. When I passed it the other day I saw that a grenade had damaged the niche housing the telescope, causing immense damage. Had the construction of the post been completed then either Jonezi or I and the telephonist would have... Kismet! Extreme values are very close to each other in war. A week ago there was the rumour we'd be going back and today our troops are up and out in an offensive strike. The advance is underway. The Russian infantry has abandoned their positions across from ours and is retreating with our troops on their heels. Everything happened in just minutes. We're waiting for orders and will probably engage either today or tomorrow at the latest.

11 August 1917

We're all alone on our hilltop now. All the troops have gone following the enemy. When it was established that the front positions of the Russians had been evacuated, I couldn't resist wanting to confirm myself that it was so. I and a few other adventure-loving companions went to pay a visit. We took off in the afternoon and climbed over our as well as enemy wire entanglements. This caused damages to both body and clothes but we were able to jump into the enemy position. The Russians left quite a number of things even though their retreat was not a hasty one. My telephonist took possession of some welcome leftovers. We dragged with us bread, rusks, potatoes, canned food, etc. bowls, tent beds, soap and God knows what else. I only took 2 tarpaulins that I desperately needed. We still had to be on the jump in case of an eventual Russian patrol. We finally started back towards home and arrived at our station when nightfall broke in. As we only received our scanty rations for dinner, these spoils were much appreciated and devoured that same evening. As we hadn't received orders to join the battery we set off next morning in search of food on the other side. We took off early in the morning and quickly found cans of food, corn, bread etc. When we reached one of the Russian mountain positions we suddenly had this magnificent view of Romania. The sun was just rising; there wasn't even a breeze, just complete silence. Anyone not part of these belligerent pursuits would not have been able to guess that there were dead bodies and wounded soldiers lying in these mountains. Once back home we received the orders to break up camp and report for duty. The advance was underway. Our successes are fantastic.

15 August 1917

Having been recalled we now set off on a strenuous march in order to reach our group. No one said a word except our First Lieutenant who got us ready for dispatch. He said he was satisfied with us. I received orders the very next day to collect ammunition and deliver it to a 15cm battery. And so we set out in our fully loaded vehicles in search of where the battery could be, driving through a territory that had been occupied by the enemy only a few days earlier. There was great confusion in the advance. The Gjtoz is a very narrow valley. Ammunition, food provisions and soldier trains were driving along in compact formation. On both sides of the road you could see columns of undercarriages, a site for dressing wounds, an exhausted infantry division, a portable forge, etc. in an inextricable pell-mell formation. In between the carriage resting places there were also batteries from the smallest to the largest calibres – old and new models all one next to the other. Then howitzers, telescopes, cannons, a 30cm mortar in a small gully. The German 2cm mortar stood alone on the side of the road and filled the valley with its rumbling. We carried on in our vehicles. The road was covered with 10cm of dust. The heavy traffic had rummaged it up turning the entire valley into one big dustbin all the way up to the mountain tops. We got to a bend in the road where we suddenly were spied upon by the enemy. An enemy plane was flying over us. We sensed that something was about to happen. We flew past milestones and parapets at top speed. No sooner had we passed this dangerous part of the road when we heard a grenade barrage exploding where we had just passed. We reached the battery and unloaded. We were hidden by a steep slope but the plane still kept circling above us. We turned around and waited a while till the plane had gone. This beastly insect finally disappeared behind a mountain – we carried on. The scoundrel must have seen us just as we passed the bridge from before and started throwing grenades and shrapnel one after the other at us. We sat like mice in the front seat, our heads sunk deep into our shoulders. There was that much dust so that one could hardly see anything of the road. Shots flew past near us. Then there was the screeching of shrapnel bullets. Our own batteries were firing shots. And yet you could still hear your hearts beating. On we went. The dust penetrated our pores, accumulated up our noses, eyes, ears so that we couldn't see the road. And yet we drove on at high speed as though it was a question of life and death. We finally reached a bend in the road behind a protective slope – we were safe. I counted the heads of my dear companions. Thank goodness no one was hurt. And so we slowly drove back home. I got reassigned to a telephone line substation which serviced the observation posts of the infantry. I slept in the tent. That will do as long as it doesn't rain. The offensive was halted, probably due to insufficient preparation and too little artillery ammunition. I hope that mistake can be rectified in time.

21 August 1917

Life at this substation is quite nice, not too strenuous and one has plenty of time on one's hand. But all that will all end in 1-2 days because there's news of me being shifted out to the infantry. Things are twice as dangerous now in this half and half mobile and trench warfare. I won't have any cover there from an enemy barrage. I'm getting a bit worried again. If only I had already been made a *Fähnrich*. Then there would be an end of one sitting at the battery command and the other on the infantry observation post. Away from the battery where the captain's every order usually comes with the comment "or else you'll be locked up". I'm not asking to get better treatment as an officer than when I was a cadet. I'd prefer being with the cadre. Oh well, the bondage of being a cadet will pass in time and someone higher up will protect me as artillery-infantryman. I get the same feeling like just before going to the dentist. Back then I was comforted with the words, "you're not getting your head cut off". Out there, however, that could well be the case.

28 August 1917

I was allowed to go to the parking lot instead of with the advance party. I was also allowed a few days' rest. I hardly could believe my ears! I received the order after two days to lay a cable to the infantry. An observation post needed to be established. We were supposed to set railway stations and other important points (Tirgarl-ocuas???) on fire with our 21cm mortar. The cable was laid by late in the night. We wrapped ourselves in our blankets and slept beautifully in our little hollow despite the attack on one of our neighbouring infantry positions. Firing at the railway stations began in the morning with the roadbed being hit. The eastern section and the adjacent timber yard began burning in the afternoon. By nightfall the entire eastern horizon was ablaze and we could see it all the way back home. A difficult time for me followed: aimless rushing back and forth with everyone mocking whoever was frantically running around; changing of orders ten times in a row which isn't conducive to building trust in the leadership; horrifically unfair insults in front of the telephonists followed by the leader's confession of having been wrong, etc. Oh, August 1917, I shall often think of this day in the future.

I've been terribly homesick these days. Although still of a young age, life has grabbed me in the roughest way. The letters from my parents are always comforting and make me feel better as do my dreams of the future and of becoming a forest manager. However, I have now written to my future benefactor, Uncle Fery, and will passionately study photo chemistry in future. Having been on the observation post up to the middle of September I have received a quiet position as commander of a telephone exchange and am hoping to be soon nominated for the grade of *Fähnrich.*

Today is the 16th of September. After 4 months of field duty I have finally received the 'Bronze Button'. Should I rejoice if that other *Fähnrich* (who was never with the infantry but only about 8 full days on the observation post) received the 2nd Class Silver Button? While my other companions and I did 1-month duty in the field he was recovering from his "Gentleman's sickness" after just that one short stint. What does the metal button matter to me? All I care about is leaving this battery but being a *Fähnrich* now means I will have to stick with it. I want to get away from the battery because of the thing with throwing grenades. The nobility of being with a battery won't change anything except for the relationship between the officers among themselves and towards the cadets. I hope a benevolent star will help me get away from here. All I want is to stay healthy and get back home in one piece. Nothing else matters.

25 September 1917

A lot has changed. My battery was ordered to leave during the night. I was transferred to the 15cm Longhorn which makes me very happy. Away from the conceited pack around the mortars that use you till you're bleeding and treat you like an animal. There at least I will get officer's rations from day one and will be treated in a friendly manner so that I'll wonder if I'm dreaming. But to counter all this there is devastating news. The fine "pack" from the mortar battery took my suitcase including my shoes, blanket, etc., and now here comes the big blow: I just received the bad news that our service time as cadets has been increased from 4 to 8 months. I can now start from scratch again with the hope of getting a mention for a promotion not before the beginning of 1918. I'm quite shattered. Why does fate want to punish me like this? Enough now for a long time. I'll try to get over this blow. What is so demoralising is that I can't lift a little finger to change anything. Farewell Diary… for a long time!

1 October 1917

I'm having a great time at my cannon where I'm stationed. The officers treat me like a human being – no comparison with those at the mortars. I'm comfortably sitting in the officers' quarters, awaiting my promotion and becoming a *Fähnrich.*

8 October 1917

Finally! Finally! I have at last been made a *Fähnrich.* I did have to look after matters myself, otherwise I might not have arrived at where I am now and perhaps not for a long time. During one of my duty trips to Berezk, I went to see the corps office to ask about our promotions and what do you know, we had already been listed as *Fähnrichs* for a fortnight now. I have now been given the grade of provisions supply officer and drive around to Brassó and surrounding areas to purchase things for my battery - a very pleasurable duty. Being able to see the Asian inspired ruins and the beautiful landscapes of Transylvania is very nice indeed. If only I were able to send some of the stockpiles from here back home. Life looks a lot different when you have a full belly. I would love to stay here, but I think not much will come of that. I will be granted days off by the cadre but where to after that? I hope not to the mine throwers!

12 Novembr 1917

Before you know it you're in with the cadre. But Krakow…. That's where Beuger and I had to go before ending up in Pest because the cannons belonged to the 2nd Regiment. After 4 "black" days I arrived in Vienna and Straßnitz for half a day then to Pest from where I immediately got sent on 17 days' holiday. I won't stay with the cadre for long. It's not very nice there… lots of people I don't know. But where to and why?

His mother, Marie Papesch née Hrdliczka added the following note, supposedly on 29 April 1947:

"My poor child, what anguish, suffering and homesickness your young little heart had to suffer only to finally die such a horrendous death on 29/IV 1947 as a result of the strenuous years of war.

3. List of Themes

T.1. Architecture-1

T.2. Architecture-2

T.3. Architecture

T.4. Monument

T.5. House in the countyside of Wörschach

T.6. Cat

T.7. Composition with portrait

T.8. Winter landscape

T.9. Nature

T.10. Dual portrait

T.11. Peilstein-1

T.12. Peilstein-2

T.13. Summer portrait-1

T.14. Summer portrait-2

T.15. Portrait of Ottokar Papesch

T.16. View towards the outside-1

T.17. View towards the outside-2

T.18. Summer sport

T.19. Streetscape

T.20. Portrait with animals-1

T.21. Portrait with animals-2

T.22. Winter landscape-1

T.23. Winter landscape-2

T.24. Winter sport-1

T.25. Winter sport-2

T.26. Interieur

4. List of Drawings

S.1: Boat

S.2: Farm house

S.3: Molly the dog (drawn by my 13-year-old father, 1911)

S.4: War year 1915

S.5: Wounded soldier

S.6: Soldiers on a sled

S.7: At sea

S.8: Sailboats

S.9: Ships-1

S.10: Ships-2

S.11: Ships-3

S.12: Submarine and Zeppelin

S.13: Sailboats

5. My Father's Will

In the case of my death, I hereby nominate both my children, Peter and Christa, as my heirs. The division of the inheritance is to be executed as follows: the jewellery in my possession being 1 large and one small bracelet, 1 wristwatch and 1 ring should go to my daughter, Christa, in its entirety. This jewellery is to remain in my wife's trust until my daughter, Christa, has become of age. My wife is to receive my half of the property at Bellariastrasse 22, Vienna 19, with the proviso that my parents' residency at Eichelhofstrasse 2 be secured for as long as they live. As she is half owner of that house, she shall not dispute my parents' right whether directly or indirectly. My parents must be given an appropriate room, especially during the winter months. The room next to the terrace is not suitable unless the heating is either repaired or completely replaced. I leave the right of residency in the house of Eichelhofstrasse 2, Vienna 19, to my beloved parents who lost their apartment during the bombings of the war. My children, who will inherit my half of the house, must respect this, my will. My stamp collection is to be returned to my father who laid its foundation stones. It will then be up to him whether to divide the collection between his grandchildren or whether to leave it to Peter entirely once he has become of age. Should my brother show any interest on behalf of his son, Roger (which has not been the case so far despite my having asked on several occasions), I would suggest that Peter get the Austrian and European parts and Roger the foreign countries of the collection.

Lainz, April 1947
Dr Otto Papesch [sic]

Addendum

There is a deposit of 15,000 Schillings in a savings account in Czechia. This amount is to go to my parents in a first instance. Should they wish to move there, they can make use of those funds as they require. The remainder shall go in equal parts to my wife and my two children. The contents of my jewellery cabinet (the canister, gold coins and gold pieces) shall go to my son, Peter, but are entrusted to my wife until he comes of age.

Lainz, April 1947
Dr Otto Papesch [sic]

6. Photographic Album of the Invasion of Poland 1939

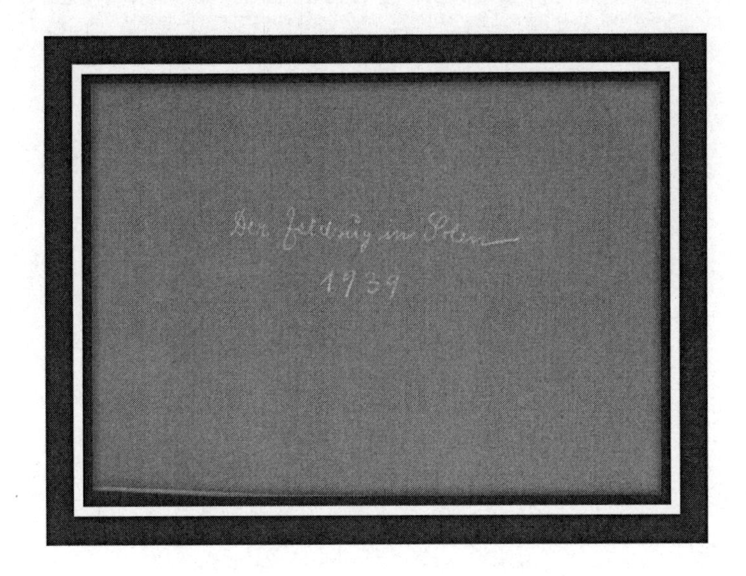

PhAP. Cover of the photo album, Poland, 1939

PhAP1. al: and ar: Lazy days in Partschendorf;
bl: 2 soldiers; br: Sunday school out of door

PhAP2. al: Two columns marching to the water; ar: First commandment: Order!; bl: Bathing idyll; br: In the swell of the weir

PhAP3. All four photos: The last days of summer

PhAP4. Title: Off we go!; al: In step; ar: Crossing the border at Zamojce; bl: What's the trouble up front?; br: The first refugees

PhAP5.Title: The two phases of Polish roads; al and ar: Horrendous dust; bl and br: and the reverse

PhAP6. Title: The advance; al: The blasted bridge near Bielitz [Bielsko-Biala]; ar: Congested roads; bl: Farmboys on country roads; br: Advancing under cover

PhAP7. Title: The face of war; al: The bridge near Teschen [Cieszyn]; ar: Greetings from above; bl: The ruins of Krasnobród; br: First attempts at reconstruction

PhAP8. al: The detachment before Krakow; ar: Great camouflage; bl: The boss's office; br: Admonitions and warnings

PhAP9. Title: Keeping up one's skills; al: Tailor; ar: Coiffeur; bl: Cleanliness at all costs; br: Dental hygiene

PhAP10. al and ar: Friendly country folk; bl: Peaceful village life; br: News service

PhAP11. al: Snipers suddenly start shooting; ar: ...and the ensuing punishment; bl: Our first prisoners; br: Endless columns being evacuated

PhAP12. [Empty page with only a photo of my father with his camera]

PhAP13. al: Sunny bivouac; ar: ...with the Polish march blasting on the radio; bl: Wireless news service; br: Skat outdoors

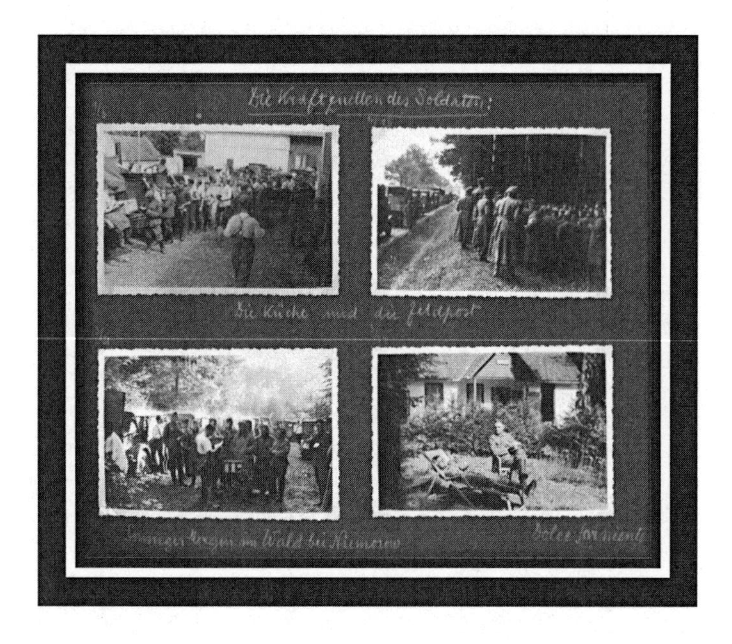

PhAP14. Title: The source of military strength; al: and ar: Meals and mail; bl: Sunny morning in the forest near Niemorow; br: Dolce far niente

PhAP15. Title: Enormous spoils; al: English-Polish tank; ar: Light artillery; bl: Heavy artillery; br: Polish 22cm mortar.

PhAP16. al: Looted petrol store; ar: Polish anti-aircraft gun; bl: Blown-up artillery; br: Polish artillery warehouse

PhAP17. al and ar: The big soccer match; bl and br: And the spectators

PhAP18. No captions for the top pictures. al: Otto and soldiers leaning against a vehicle; ar: Polish soldiers; bl: Little chooks; br: Guest performance inside the bomber

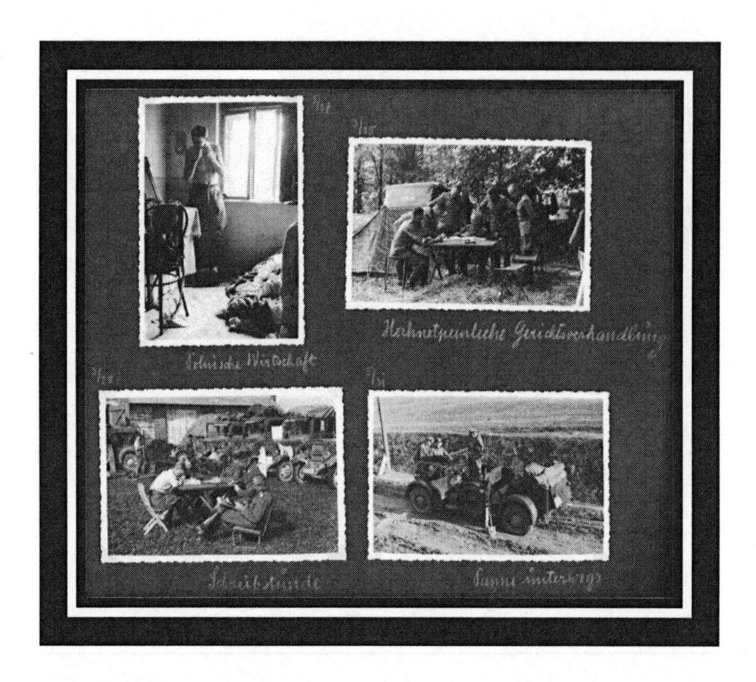

PhAP19. al: Polish housekeeping; ar: Scrutinising judicial hearing; bl: Time for writing letters; br: Breakdown along the road

PhAP20. al: Reporting for duty, sir; ar: Early morning wash at the well; bl. & br.: Idyllic moments in the countryside

PhAP21. al: A hungry fellow; ar: Expert appraisal; bl: Oh yea… the beer sure was good!; br: Officer with dog (no caption provided)

PhAP22. al: Weapons cleaning; ar: Right turn!; bl: Morning fog; br: A small traffic accident

PhAP23. al: Old school chums; ar: Precious game; bl: K.d.F. (Kraft durch Freude) [Strength Through Joy] in Poland; br: WH51033

PhAP24. al: Never-ending columns of prisoners; ar: A soldier's fate; bl: View across the border along the San River; br: Tragic homecoming

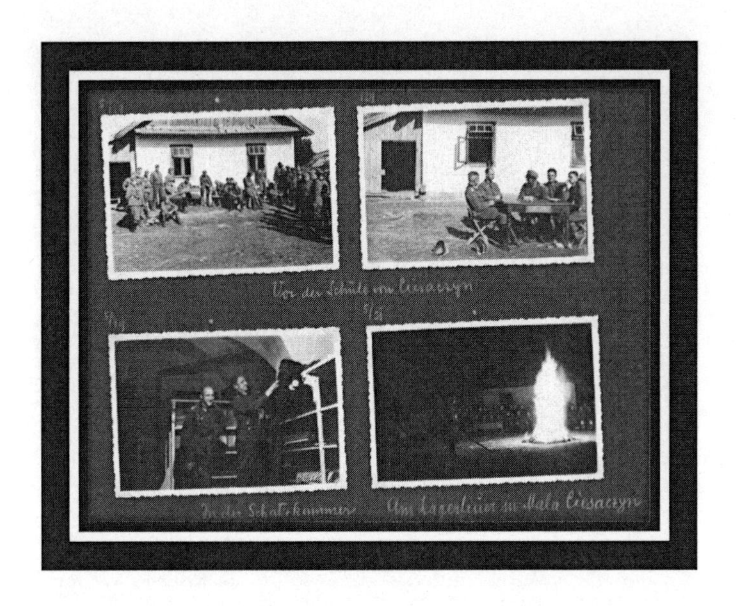

PhAP25. al and ar: In front of the school in Ciesaczyn; bl: In the treasure vault; br: Around the bonfire in Mala Ciesaczyn

PhAP26. al and ar: Crossover into Russian territory; bl: Wanderers returning from Jaroslau; br: First encounter with the Russians

PhAP27. al: In Polish mud; ar: Russians requisitioning straw; bl: Near the bridge of... [no further caption]; br: German-Russian palaver

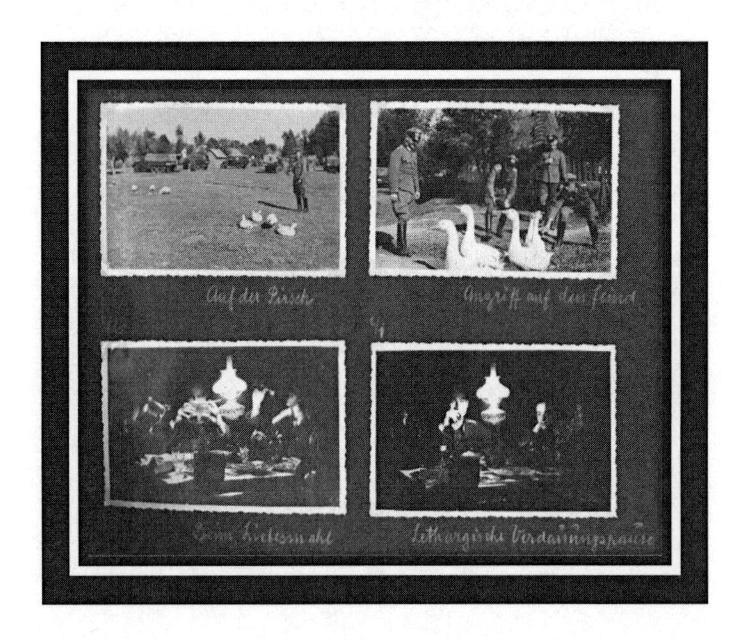

PhAP28. al: Hunting; ar: Attacking the enemy; bl: The communal banquet; br: A lethargic interval while digesting

PhAP29. al and ar: Counsels of the future; bl: Country quarters; br: Rear view mirror shot

PhAP30. al: Podklastrze; ar: Airborne bomb in the thicket; bl and br: The Polish escape route in the forest of Tomaszow

PhAP31. Title: Enormous spoils

PhAP32. al: Looking for loot; ar: Along the Vistula; bl and br: The big pontoon bridge across the Vistula River

PhAP33. al: Arrival in the Jewish village; ar: Quite a commotion; bl and br: Everyone wants to bargain straight off

PhAP34. Title: The Ghetto of Tarlow

PhAP35. al and ar: Their favourite occupation; bl: The bedbugs of Tarlow; br: Two special representatives of the chosen people

PhAP36. al, ar and bl: Noble quarters; br: Just before Warsaw

PhAP37. Title: Marching into Warsaw

7. List of Illustrations

Otto Papesch Biogaphy
List of Illustrations

Front piece: Otto Papesch aged 38 years

Chapter I

1. Otto Papesch at the age of 38 (a rare photo where he is seen smiling), 1936
2. Peter and Emilie Hrdliczka (my father's maternal grandparents)
3. The Grebner family crest in one of the stained-glass windows of the Church of Saint Sebaldus in Nuremberg
4. The Hrdliczkas. From left to right: Peter, Emilie, Marie and Viktor; back row from left to right: Paul, Max, Ferdinand, Leopold and Gustav
5. The von Grebner family crest
6. Ferdinand Hrdliczka (Fery) (1860-1942)

7. Viktor Hrdliczka with his wife, Marie (née Alder, nicknamed Maus) and their children (l. to r.): Viktor, Gertrude, Martha
8. Max Hrdliczka (1865-1958)
9. The Papesch, Hrdliczka and Alder families in the Prater, 1907. Otto is out on the right beside his father, Ottokar Papesch.
10. Marie Hrdliczka just before her wedding in February 1898
11. The young Ottokar Papesch about to marry his sweetheart "Maritischi" in February 1898
12. Pragerstraße in the 3rd Viennese District seen from the Franzens Bridge

Chapter II

13. Almanac of 1898
14. The page for November in the Almanac of 1898
15. The symbols and their meaning in the Almanac of 1898
16. My father's birth and christening certificate, 1904
17. Certified copy of my father's birth and christening certificate of 27 September 1938
18. Otto Papesch, barely two months old
19. The proud Mum ("Maritschi" as she was called by her relatives and friends) with her Otti (as my father was called in family circles), 1899
20. The proud parents with their son smiling into the camera, 1901
21. 3-year-old Otto with his proud parents, 1901
22. Otto with his dad, Ottokar, 1902
23. Otto, 1903
24. 8-year-old Otto, 1906
25. Otto and his brother Vicki, 1907
26. Otto and Vicki, 1908
27. Otto and Vicki, 1909
28. "Three men". Ottokar and his sons, Otto and Vicki, in the summer of 1909
29. Otto and Vicki, 1912
30. Otto with a deer fawn, 1915
31. Family outing by the river, 1909
32. Otto, Vicki and their dad sleigh-riding, 1910
33. 15-year-old Otto on horseback, 1913
34. My father's postcard to his grandmother, Emilie Hrdliczka, 1914

35. The building where my father went to school
36. My father's swimming medals, 1913
37. Reverse side of my father's swimming medals, 1913
38. My father's discus-throwing medal
39. My father was also a member of the Donauwacht sports club
40. Later in 1929, my father participated in the marathon Quer Durch *Wien*

Chapter III

41. "I give gold for iron", 1914. The iron wedding rings of Marie and Ottokar Papesch
42. My father, Vicki and their mother, 1916
43. My father with two of his pups
44. My father in uniform. He was not yet 18 years old
45. Main building of the Ludvika-Academy in Budapest, 1913
46. Széchenyi Thermal Baths in Budapest
47. My father with two other fellow cadets, 1916
48. My father's field cutlery
49. Telegram dated 3 February 1917 to Otto's parents: *Exams successfully passed. Being sent into the field on 8 February. Come quickly or send money via telegraphic transfer. Otto*
50. Map of Romania
51. My father with "Big Bertha"
52. My father near the bridge over the Brenta River. This is where the 12th Battle of the Isonzo was fought in northern Italy in 1918
53. World War I: my father (left on second row) with his troop. I don't know where

Chapter IV

54. Otto (22 years old) and Vicki (16 years old), 1920
55. Excerpts from the examination report, First State Exam, Technical University, Vienna, 1921
56. Examination report, Second State Exam, Technical University, Vienna, Years 1912/1918 to1921/1922
57. Ing. Otto Papesch certificate of citizenship, 10 October 1924

58. Failed attempt in 1924 of obtaining his doctorate
59. Letter dated 29 November 1937 certifying that my father worked on his thesis under the guidance of Dr J. M. Eder between 1924 and 1925
60. My father's doctorate certificate, 3 July 1926
61. A proud "Herr Doktor" strolling down the street, 1916

Chapter V

62. Otto, 1926
63. My father at the age of 30, 1928
64. My father's Leica
65. RAVAG lecture by Otto Papesch on photographing at night
66. RAVAG lecture by Otto Papesch on photographing during winter sport
67. RAVAG lecture by Otto Papesch on photography and criminology
68. Margarete
69. On Lake Garda
70. Winter sport
71. Puss in Boot
72. Landscape with portrait
73. Monument
74. Portrait in Wörschach
75. Spot-Rowing
76. Leisure time
77. Winter sport
78. Photographing at night
79. Experiments with shadows
80. Spring: View from the house on the Eichelhof over the Danube River and start of the Danube Canal
81. The laboratory at the Herlango firm
82. My father held a series of lectures on photography during the years 1944/45
83. My father with groups of his students

Chapter VI

84. My parents on the ski slopes of Mallnitz, 1929
85. Dürnstein taken from my father's faltboat, July 1930
86. Schönbühel taken from my father's faltboat, July 1930
87. Confirmation that my father withdrew from the Catholic Church on 24 April 1931
88. My newly-wed parents, 6 June 1931
89. Dr and Mrs Papesch
90. The living room in Rienößlgasse 22/6
91. Confirmation of my parents' domicile on the Eichelhof, 3 August 1933
92. Left: The house on the Eichelhf (view from the living room down onto the terrace); right: view of the house from the Hackhofegasse
93. The living room on the Eichelhof and the piano that my father would play on
94. My father's beloved rucksack
95. One of my father's many hiking maps
96. Newspaper article about gardening
97. Left: The garden on the Eichelhof with steps up from below; right: The upper terrace and the wall from where Frau Max called down

Chapter VII

98. My father aged 40, 1938
99. My father's citizenship certificate dated 13 March 1938
100. My father once again in uniform, 1938
101. Excerpt from the Taschen-Brockhaus-zum-Zeitgeschehen, 1940, page 77: Map of the invasion of Poland, 1939
102. Excerpt from the photo album, Poland, 1939. "The two phases of the Polish roads". Top: "Horrific dust"; Bottom: "…Or else, mud"
103. Excerpt from the photo album, Poland, 1939. Top: "The division just before Krakau"; Bottom: "Great camouflage"
104. Excerpt from the photo album, Poland, 1939. Top: "The hungry one"; Bottom: "Expert assessment"
105. Excerpt from the photo album, Poland, 1939. Top: "Two single files"; Bottom: "Gushing waters in the weir"

106. Excerpt from the photo album, Poland, 1939. Top: "Endless columns of prisoners"; Bottom: "Sad homecoming"
107. Excerpt from the photo album, Poland, 1939.
108. "Crossing over into Russian territory"
109. Excerpt from the photo album, Poland, 1939.
110. "The big pontoon bridge over the Vistula River"
111. Excerpt from the photo album, Poland, 1939. "In the Ghetto of Tarlow"
112. Excerpt from the photo album, Poland, 1939. "The march into Warsaw"
113. First Lieutenant Papesch with his camera
114. Main military register, pages 126 and 126/2
115. Military service, certificate of injury, pages 1 and 2
116. Otto Papesch discharge papers dated 14 August 1941, pages 1 and 2
117. Otto Papesch: welfare entitlement certificate dated 14 August 1941

Chapter VIII

118. My mother with her Sealyham Terrier pups
119. My mother with her favourite Sealyham Terrier named Maffy
120. My brother, Peter, with Maffy
121. My beaming mother with her 3-year-old son Peter following the return of my father from Poland
122. My father with his son, Peter, 1941
123. My mother with Peter and me, 1943
124. My father with Peter
125. Peter
126. Peter and his little sister
127. My mother, happy now with her two children
128. Brother and sister, 1945
129. My father (with the Leica under his arm) with his dad, October 1938
130. My father with his beloved mother
131. Father and son during one of their hikes
132. My father in uniform, 1916, and a soldier again in 1939. In between, the man who loved nature

Chapter IX

133. My father at the sanatorium in Grimmenstein and postcard from my grandparents to Gertrude Hofmann (née Hrdliczka), youngest daughter of Viktor Hrdliczka and my grandmother's niece
134. My father's death certificate, 8 May 1947
135. Letter from Dr F. B. Trudeau dated 16 April 1947 and my mother's note upon receiving it on the 29th of April
136. My father's grave in the Zentalfriedhof (Central cemetery) of Vienna
137. My father aged 40, 1938
138. My father's grandson, Lars Papesch Mulà, age 40, 2017
139. My father's grandson, Thor Papesch Mulà, age 40, 2017

Grebner Papesch Hrdliczka Family Chronicle

Excerpts from the Grebner Papesch Hrdliczka Family Chronicle:

140. Chronicle of the Grebner Papesch Hrdliczka Family (my grandfather's handwritten booklet)
141. Chronicle of the Grebner Papesch Hrdliczka Family: Excerpt from the 1676 family register 1)
142. Chronicle of the Grebner Papesch Hrdliczka Family: Franz von Grebner
143. Chronicle of the Grebner Papesch Hrdliczka Family: Ferdinand Hrdliczka
144. Chronicle of the Grebner Papesch Hrdliczka Family: Max Hrdliczka
145. Chronicle of the Grebner Papesch Hrdliczka Family: Viktor Hrdliczka (father), Marie Alder and Martha Hrdliczka
146. Chronicle of the Grebner Papesch Hrdliczka Family: Viktor Hrdliczka (son)
147. Chronicle of the Grebner Papesch Hrdliczka Family: Gertrud Hrdliczka
148. Chronicle of the Grebner Papesch Hrdliczka Family: Emilie Grebner and Eduard Papesch
149. Emilie Grebner (1841-1926)
150. Eduard Papesch (1835-88)
151. Chronicle of the Grebner Papesch Hrdliczka Family: Ottokar Papesch and Marie Hrdliczka
152. Chronicle of the Grebner Papesch Hrdliczka Family: Otto Papesch and Margarete Pirquet

153. Chronicle of the Grebner Papesch Hrdliczka Family: Viktor Papesch and Mary Marczyk

My father's war-time: 17 February to 12 November 1917

154. My father's notebook: "Otto Papesch First Year at Feotz 3 Budapest VII. Hajtsar Nt 22"

Themes

1. Architecture-1
2. Architecture-2
3. Architecture
4. Monument
5. House in the countryside of Wörschach
6. Cat
7. Composition with portrait
8. Winter landscape
9. Nature
10. Double portrait
11. The municipality of Peilstein
12. The surroundings of Peilstein
13. Summer portrait-1
14. Summer portrait-2
15. Portrait of Ottokar Papesch
16. View out-1
17. View out-2
18. Summer sport
19. Street scape
20. Portrait with animals-1
21. Portrait with animals-2
22. Winter landscape-1
23. Winter landscape-2
24. Winter sport-1
25. Winter sport-2
26. Interieur

Sketchbook

1. Boat
2. Farm house
3. Molly the dog (drawn by 13-year-old Otto)
4. Year 1915 of the war
5. Wounded soldier
6. Soldiers on a sled
7. At sea
8. Sailboats
9. Ships-1
10. Ships-2
11. Ships-3
12. Submarine and Zeppelin
13. Sailboats

Photo Album, Poland, 1939

Each sheet is identified with PhAP and numbered (above left = al; above right = ar; below left = bl; below right = br)

PhAP. The cover of the photo album, Poland, 1939
PhAP1. al: and ar: *Lazy days in Partschendorf*;
bl: *2 soldiers*; br: *Sunday school out of doors*
PhAP2. al: *Two columns marching to the water*; ar: *First commandment: Order!*; bl: *Bathing idyll*; br: *In the swell of the weir*
PhAP3. All four photos: *The last days of summer*
PhAP4. Title: *Off we go!*; al: *In step*; ar: *Crossing the border at Zamojce*; bl: *What's the trouble up front?*; br: *The first refugees*
PhAP5. Title: *The two phases of Polish roads*; al and ar: *Horrendous dust*; bl and br: *and the reverse*
PhAP6. Title: *The advance*; al: *The blasted bridge near Bielitz [Bielsko-Biala]*; ar: *Congested roads*; bl: *Farmboys on country roads*; br: *Advancing under cover*
PhAP7. Title: *The face of war*; al: *The bridge near Teschen [Cieszyn]*; ar: *Greetings from above*; bl: *The ruins of Krasnobród*; br: *First attempts at reconstruction*

PhAP8. al: *The detachment before Krakow*; ar: *Great camouflage*; bl: *The boss's office*; br: *Admonitions and warnings*

PhAP9. Title: *Keeping up one's skills*; al: *Tailor*; ar: *Coiffeur*; bl: *Cleanliness at all costs*; br: *Dental hygiene*

PhAP10. al and ar: *Friendly country folk*; bl: *Peaceful village life*; br: *News service*

PhAP11. al: *Snipers suddenly start shooting*; ar: *...and the ensuing punishment*; bl: *Our first prisoners*; br: *Endless columns being evacuated*

PhAP12. *[Empty page with only a photo of my father with his camera. See below.]*

PhAP13. al: *Sunny bivouac*; ar: *...with the Polish march blasting on the radio*; bl: *Wireless news service*; br: *Skat outdoors*

PhAP14. Title: *The source of military strength*; al: and ar: *Meals and mail;* bl: *Sunny morning in the forest near Niemorow;* br: *Dolce far niente*

PhAP15. Title: *Enormous spoils;* al: *English-Polish tank;* ar: *Light artillery;* bl: *Heavy artillery;* br: *Polish 22cm mortar.*

PhAP16. al: *Looted petrol store;* ar: *Polish anti-aircraft gun;* bl: *Blown-up artillery;* br: *Polish artillery warehouse*

PhAP17. al and ar: *The big soccer match;* bl and br: *And the spectators*

PhAP18. No captions for the top pictures. al: *Otto and soldiers leaning against a vehicle;* ar: *Polish soldiers;* bl: *Little chooks;* br: *Guest performance inside the bomber*

PhAP19. al: *Polish housekeeping;* ar: *Scrutinising judicial hearing;* bl: *Time for writing letters;* br: *Breakdown along the road*

PhAP20. al: *"Reporting for duty, sir";* ar: *"Early morning wash at the well";* bl. & br.: *"Idyllic moments in the countryside"*

PhAP21. al: *A hungry fellow;* ar: *Expert appraisal;* bl: *Oh yea...the beer sure was good!;* br: Officer with dog (no caption provided)

PhAP22. al: *Weapons cleaning;* ar: *Right turn!;* bl: *Morning fog;* br: *A small traffic accident*

PhAP23. al: *Old school chums;* ar: *Precious game;* bl: *K.d.F. (Kraft durch Freude) [Strength Through Joy] in Poland;* br: *WH51033*

PhAP24. al: *Never-ending columns of prisoners;* ar: *A soldier's fate;* bl: *View across the border along the San River;* br: *Tragic homecoming*

PhAP25. al and ar: *In front of the school in Ciesaczyn;* bl: *In the treasure vault;* br: *Around the bonfire in Mala Ciesaczyn*

PhAP26. al and ar: *Crossover into Russian territory;* bl: *Wanderers returning from Jaroslau;* br: *First encounter with the Russians*
PhAP27. al: *In Polish mud;* ar: *Russians requisitioning straw;* bl: *Near the bridge of... [no further caption];* br: *German-Russian palaver*
PhAP28. al: *Hunting;* ar: *Attacking the enemy;* bl: *The communal banquet;* br: *A lethargic interval while digesting*
PhAP29. al and ar: *Counsels of the future;* bl: *Country quarters;* br: *Rear view mirror shot*
PhAP30. al: *Podklastrze;* ar: *Airborne bomb in the thicket;* bl and br: *The Polish escape route in the forest of Tomaszow*
PhAP31. Title: *Enormous spoils*
PhAP32. al: *Looking for loot;* ar: *Along the Vistula;* bl and br: *The big pontoon bridge across the Vistula River*
PhAP33. al: *Arrival in the Jewish village;* ar: *Quite a commotion;* bl and br: *Everyone wants to bargain straight off*
PhAP34. Title: *The Ghetto of Tarlow*
PhAP35. al and ar: *Their favourite occupation;* bl: *The bedbugs of Tarlow;* br: *Two special representatives of the chosen people*
PhAP36. al, ar and bl: *Noble quarters;* br: *Just before Warsaw*
PhAP37. Title: *Marching into Warsaw*